MALCOLM·HILLIER'S
CHRISTMAS

MALCOLM·HILLIER'S
CHRISTMAS

Photography by
DIANA MILLER

BARNES
&NOBLE
BOOKS
NEW YORK

A DORLING KINDERSLEY BOOK

First American Edition, 1992

This edition published by Barnes & Noble, Inc.,
by arrangement with Dorling Kindersley

2000 Barnes & Noble Books

M 10 9 8 7 6 5 4 3 2 1

ISBN 0-7607-2329-X

Published in the United States by
Dorling Kindersley, Inc., 232 Madison Avenue
New York, New York 10016

Library of Congress Catalog Card Number 92-6541

Library of Congress Cataloging-in-Publication Data

Hillier, Malcolm.
    [Christmas]
    Malcolm Hillier's Christmas. -- 1st American ed.
        p.   cm.
    Includes Index.
    ISBN 1-56458-099-7
    1. Christmas. 2. Christmas decorations. 3. Christmas cookery.
I. Title. II. Title: Christmas.
GT4985.H54 1992
394.2'68282--dc20   92-6541
                                                           CIP

PROJECT EDITOR
Susan Thompson

ART EDITOR
Pauline Bayne

MANAGING EDITOR
Mary-Clare Jerram

MANAGING ART EDITOR
Gill Della Casa

U.S. EDITOR
Jeanette Mall

PRODUCTION CONTROLLER
Meryl Silbert

Typeset by
The Cooling Brown
Partnership,
London

Text film output by
The Right Type, London

Reproduced by
Colourscan, Singapore

Printed and bound by
L. Rex,
China

CONTENTS

INTRODUCTION

Christmas is the festival that appeals to the child in all of us. It is a time of great joy, new beginnings, and hope, and, for me, it has always been the most exciting time of the year. Christmas is also a time for giving and receiving, for welcoming and entertaining, and for celebrating with wonderful food and flowers.

I have always adored presents. They are wonderful to give and splendid to receive, but they are not always easy to choose. Despite the best intentions, I have never been good at finding presents in advance. Although I do have one well-prepared friend who has been known to buy presents in the week after Christmas for the following year, I think most of us are in-efficient at finding gifts, rushing around at the last minute with lists we forget to use. Fortunately handmade gifts will always be treasured by friends and family, so there are many simple ideas here for gifts that you can make well in advance of Christmas, provided you are organized!

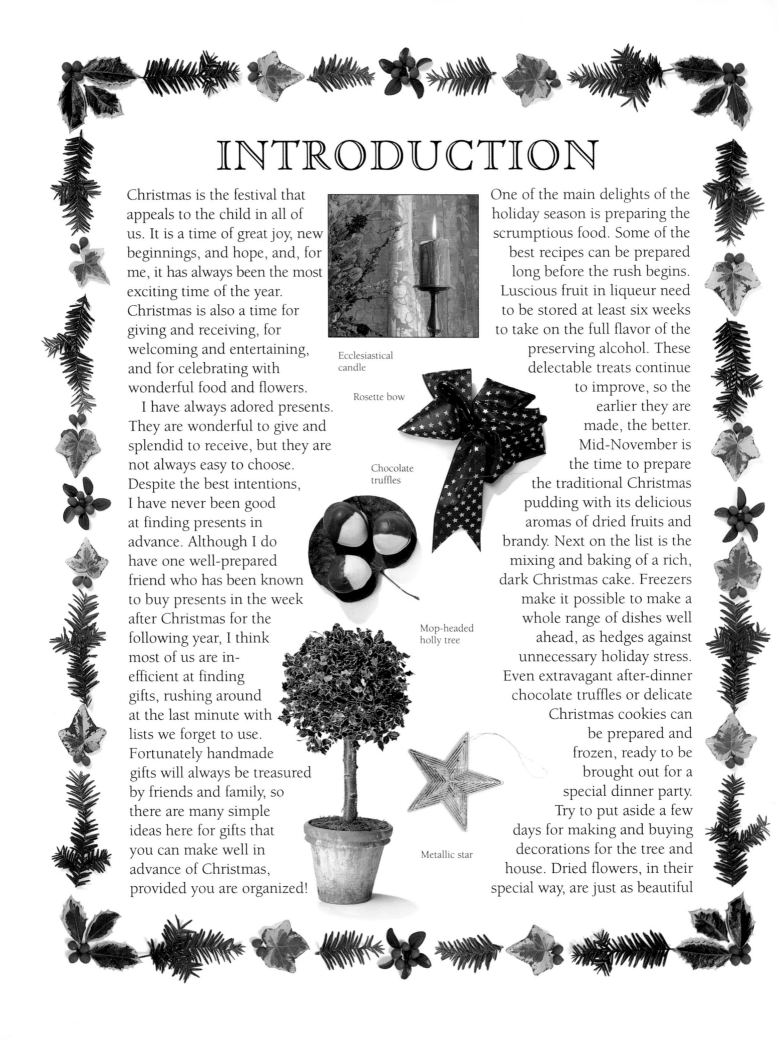

Ecclesiastical candle

Rosette bow

Chocolate truffles

Mop-headed holly tree

Metallic star

One of the main delights of the holiday season is preparing the scrumptious food. Some of the best recipes can be prepared long before the rush begins. Luscious fruit in liqueur need to be stored at least six weeks to take on the full flavor of the preserving alcohol. These delectable treats continue to improve, so the earlier they are made, the better. Mid-November is the time to prepare the traditional Christmas pudding with its delicious aromas of dried fruits and brandy. Next on the list is the mixing and baking of a rich, dark Christmas cake. Freezers make it possible to make a whole range of dishes well ahead, as hedges against unnecessary holiday stress. Even extravagant after-dinner chocolate truffles or delicate Christmas cookies can be prepared and frozen, ready to be brought out for a special dinner party. Try to put aside a few days for making and buying decorations for the tree and house. Dried flowers, in their special way, are just as beautiful as fresh flowers, and can be arranged well in advance of the festivities. Buy your fresh flowers when they are in peak condition so that they will look perfect when you are entertaining.

The focal point of Christmas is, of course, the tree. Children of all ages are thrilled by its magic. Spruce trees will often drop their needles within a few days of being cut. Despite this, I am very fond of their aromatic scent; it transports me back to my childhood and to the wild hope that there would be snow outside on Christmas Day. Christmas trees are now being cultivated to grow in a regular, full shape and to retain their needles longer after being cut. My preference is to decorate the tree and put up the other decorations just three or four days before Christmas. This is immense fun and everyone can join in to make this a family event. Of course, if you are giving early parties, the decorating will need to be done sooner.

When I was a child, Christmas Eve was the night for wrapping presents. We were always so excited that it seemed we didn't sleep at all.

Detail of evergreen arrangement

Sushi buffet

Bread wreath

Potpourri

Christmas orchids

The next morning, Father Christmas would appear very early to wake us up. Then the feverish opening of the presents in the stockings at the ends of our beds began. The presents under the tree were much squeezed and shaken during the day, but we were only allowed to open them once the Christmas cake had been cut at tea time. By the time I was a teenager, we began to have our dinner in the evening, which left time for us to go to a morning church service, have a light lunch, and then spend the afternoon preparing the feast. Each year the main course alternated between goose and roast beef. The real high point, though, was always the great array of desserts. There were always at least four, beginning with a small serving of Christmas pudding with brandy butter and ending with a refreshing compote of caramelized oranges. I still feature a large selection of desserts to bring my favorite meal of the year to a satisfying conclusion. Once Christmas is over and calm descends, I look forward to the changing seasons and all the Christmases to come.

Chapter One

EARLY
PREPARATIONS

TWO MONTHS before Christmas, it takes
willpower to start preparing gifts, decorations,
and food for the big day, but it is well worth it.
Finishing some jobs early and planning the rest,
makes life much easier in the hectic days before
Christmas. You can make imaginative presents of
potpourri, candles, dried-flower arangements,
paper decorations, luscious liqueur fruit,
Christmas puddings, and a spectacular
cake while there is still plenty of
time to work at your leisure.

GLOWING DRIED DISPLAY
*A golden bundle of lichen-covered larch
twigs, seeding grasses, deep red roses, and Chinese
lanterns split open to form flowers stand without
a vase. Old rope, sprayed gold, holds it together.
Gilded pomegranates lie at the base.*

SCENTED GIFTS

CUSHIONS AND SACHETS make wonderful Christmas presents, especially if you use rich, festive-looking materials such as velvet or brocade. They are very easy to make, although you may prefer to buy a ready-made pillow and simply insert a sachet of potpourri between the cover and the stuffing. Spicy citrus pomanders – also easy-to-make gifts – offer another way to perfume a room, their exotic fragrance lasting for years.

PERFUMED PILLOWS
Fill a flat muslin bag with a handful of fine potpourri, and sew it to the inside of a pillow case to make a delicately scented pillow. You can easily renew the potpourri from time to time.

Glass sphere

GLASS POMANDERS
The beauty of glass pomanders is that you can enjoy the fragrance of the potpourri longer than if it were displayed in an open container, plus you can see it through the glass. This potpourri is made of fragrant rose petals, other flowers, and spices.

Red ribbon

Dried rose

Decorative edging

ROSY POMANDER
A muslin sphere tightly packed with rose potpourri, and decorated with yellow, pink, and red dried roses. To preserve the colors of the roses, hang the pomander away from direct sunlight.

CITRUS POMANDERS
These delicious smelling
pomanders are straightforward
to make and they last for
years (SEE PAGE 32).

SCENTED TASSEL
When I had to restitch
this antique tassel, I put
a tablespoon of rosemary-
scented potpourri in its
padded center to make
it sweetly fragrant.

● Braiding

FRAGRANT SACHETS
To create these small sachets,
either place some potpourri in the
center of a circle of fabric and gather
the edges with ribbon, or make little
"cushions" with piped edges.

Piping ●

Tassel ●

POTPOURRIS

DELICIOUSLY PERFUMED potpourris make a perfect present. Mix your own dry or moist potpourris from fresh flowers to create more subtle and delicate fragrances than commercial potpourris. The early recipes never exuded the powerful aromas of the potpourris on sale now, and why should they? A room needs only the gentlest scent of flowers and spices to give it a special, indefinable charm.

Red rose petal

Pine cone

CHRISTMAS POTPOURRI
(Moist method)
4 cups (1 liter) partially dried
  deep red rose petals
1¼ cups (300 g) coarse salt
1 cup (250 ml) preserved ivy leaves
1 cup (250 ml) dried moss
½ cup (125 ml) Nigella orientalis seedheads
20 small pine cones
4 tbs dried juniper berries, lightly crushed
2 tbs fresh or dried mint
2 tbs ground cinnamon
2 tbs gum benzoin
4 drops lemon geranium oil
3 drops pine oil
2 drops rose oil

BLUE FLOWER POTPOURRI
(Dry method)
4 cups (1 liter) dried blue flowers such as
  larkspur, delphiniums, and hydrangeas
2 cups (500 ml) dried lemon
  verbena leaves
1 cup (250 ml) dried eucalyptus
  leaves, flowers, and seeds
1 cup (250 ml) oak moss
2 tbs ground orris root
4 drops carnation oil

Preserved ivy leaf

Nigella orientalis seedhead

Chamomile flower

Dried hops

Marigold

DRY METHOD
Mixing by the dry method makes an attractive potpourri, although the scent is not as strong as it is when made by the moist method. Mix dried fragrant flower petals, dried herbs, spices, a few drops of essential oils, and a fixative such as vetiver, ground orris root, gum benzoin, tonka beans, or frankincense. Seal in a jar and shake every day for 8 weeks, to blend the fragrances.

LATE SUMMER POTPOURRI
(Dry method)
2 cups (500 ml) dried yellow rose petals
1 cup (250 ml) dried marigolds
1 cup (250 ml) dried hops
1 cup (250 ml) dried chamomile flowers
1 tbs ground orris root
4 drops rose oil
4 drops bergamot oil

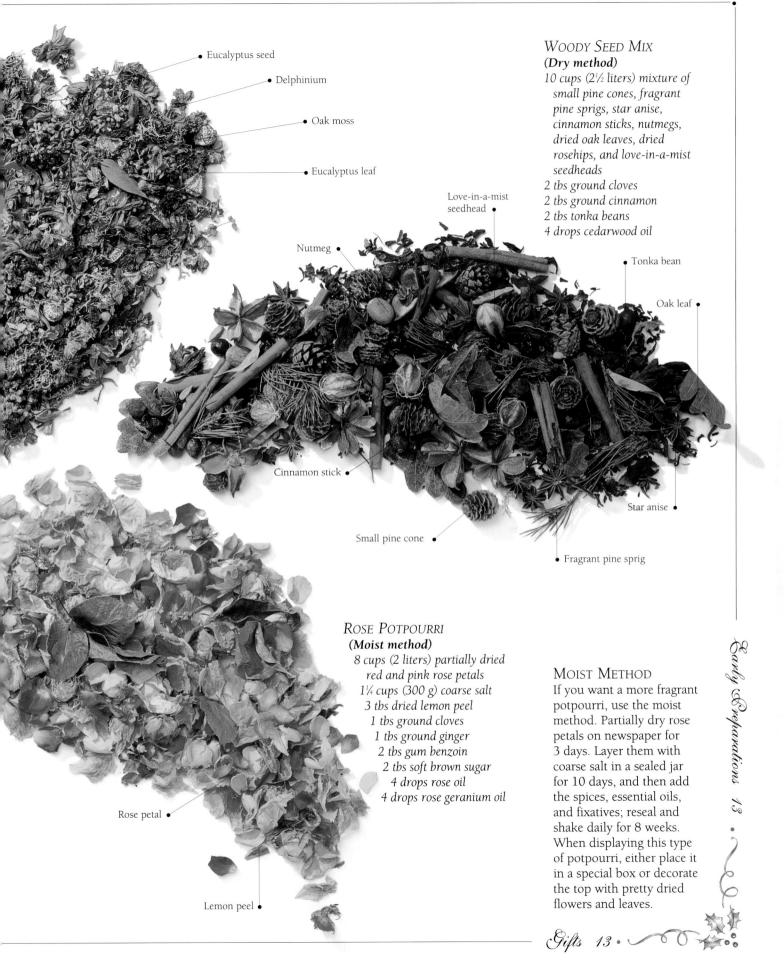

Eucalyptus seed

Delphinium

Oak moss

Eucalyptus leaf

Love-in-a-mist
seedhead

Nutmeg

Tonka bean

Oak leaf

Cinnamon stick

Star anise

Small pine cone

Fragrant pine sprig

Rose petal

Lemon peel

WOODY SEED MIX
(Dry method)
*10 cups (2½ liters) mixture of
small pine cones, fragrant
pine sprigs, star anise,
cinnamon sticks, nutmegs,
dried oak leaves, dried
rosehips, and love-in-a-mist
seedheads*
2 tbs ground cloves
2 tbs ground cinnamon
2 tbs tonka beans
4 drops cedarwood oil

ROSE POTPOURRI
(Moist method)
*8 cups (2 liters) partially dried
red and pink rose petals*
1¼ cups (300 g) coarse salt
3 tbs dried lemon peel
1 tbs ground cloves
1 tbs ground ginger
2 tbs gum benzoin
2 tbs soft brown sugar
4 drops rose oil
4 drops rose geranium oil

MOIST METHOD
If you want a more fragrant
potpourri, use the moist
method. Partially dry rose
petals on newspaper for
3 days. Layer them with
coarse salt in a sealed jar
for 10 days, and then add
the spices, essential oils,
and fixatives; reseal and
shake daily for 8 weeks.
When displaying this type
of potpourri, either place it
in a special box or decorate
the top with pretty dried
flowers and leaves.

FIERY FRUIT CANDLES

THE MENTION OF CHRISTMAS brings several images to mind – a traditional wreath on the front door, a decorated Christmas tree, fruitcake, candlelight, a roaring fire, and a country cottage with smoke curling out of the chimney, nestled between rolling fields blanketed in crisp, pure white snow. The snow is not always possible, but the other images are easy to make into reality.

Filling your home with candles creates an extra special atmosphere, soft and beautiful. Candlelight creates an environment that is cozy and welcoming, kind, and exciting, too. Although the stores are full of candles, you can create a spectacular table centerpiece by making these lifelike, fruit-shaped candles yourself. An arrangement of fruit candles combined with real fruit in a decorative basket forms an unusual and beautiful decoration, which you could also give as a present.

Apple candle •

Candle of grapes •

Elaeagnus leaf •

WHAT YOU NEED
2 tbs (28 ml) cooking oil
4 fruit-shaped molds
Darning needle
Four 10 in (25 cm) wicks
Four 5 in (13 cm) squares
of cardboard
4 glasses
4 sticks
20 oz (570 g) paraffin wax
Cooking thermometer
Orange, yellow, and
green dyes
Citronella scent
Wicker basket
Real fruit

Orange •

Lemon •

MOLDED FRUIT CANDLES

MAKE ORANGE, LEMON, APPLE, and grape candles from molds, then display them with real fruit.

1 Oil the mold. Thread the needle with the wick. Pierce the top of the mold from the inside. Thread the wick through, leaving 1 in (2.5 cm) at the top and 4 in (10 cm) at the open end.

2 Cut a collar from a cardboard square to support the mold. Place over a glass. Tie a stick to the wick and wind until taut. Heat the wax to 180° F (82° C) and add dye and scent. Fill the mold. Top off with wax after half an hour.

3 When completely cool, peel the mold from the candle. Cut the wick level at the base, and trim the top of the wick, leaving ⅜ in (1 cm) to light. Arrange in a wicker basket with real fruit.

• Wicker basket

BASKET OF FRUIT
Create a spectacular centerpiece: a basket of lemons, oranges, apples, and grapes – some real, some in the form of candles. Make several candles of each fruit so that you can replace them as they burn down, thus ensuring a display that looks its best on several occasions.

CHORUS OF CANDLES

A FLOTILLA OF COLORFUL SCENTED CANDLES floating in a clear glass bowl with their sparkling flames reflecting in the water makes a glowing table centerpiece. Fresh flowers or leaves add a finishing touch to the arrangement. On a windowsill in the same room, line up candles in old terracotta pots or put candles in tall glasses. If you make the candles well in advance, all you have to do on Christmas day is arrange and light them.

Floating candle •

• Holly leaf

FIRE ON WATER
Candles seem to shine more brightly when floating in water, especially if they are grouped in a clear or cut-glass bowl, so the flames reflect off the glass and water. Candles with flat tops and rounded bases float best.

Glass bowl •
filled with water

Candle in a Glass or Flower Pot
WHAT YOU NEED
Wicking
1 stick or pencil
20 oz (570 g) paraffin wax
1 old terracotta pot or tall glass
Cooking thermometer
Coloring
Fragrance

CANDLES IN GLASSES

Make candles in tall glass tumblers with two or three layers of different colored wax to create safe, decorative lights for a table, mantelpiece, or shelf. Allow each layer of wax to solidify before adding the next.

MOLDED CANDLES

PRIME THE WICKS (STEP 1) for homemade candles. Don't choose too thick a wick or it will smoke.

1 *Tie a length of wick, measuring about 1 in (2.5 cm) longer than the candle mold or container, to a stick or a pencil. Paint melted wax onto the wick and pull it straight. Leave it to set.*

2 *Suspend the wick inside the mold. Trim so that it almost touches the base of the mold or container. Heat the wax to 180° F (82° C), then add the coloring and fragrance. Pour into the mold. When solid, trim the wick to ⅜ in (1 cm).*

• Glass tumbler

FLOWERPOT CANDLES

Old straight-sided terracotta pots make excellent containers for candles. Before you pour in the wax, make sure the pots are clean, and block the drainage holes with adhesive clay. Add a drop of your favorite fragrance to the wick to give the candles a scent.

Terracotta pot •

PATTERNED TISSUE PAPER

MUCH OF THE WRAPPING PAPER available in specialty stores is very expensive, and often rather boring. I prefer to make my own, using humble tissue paper. Inexpensive, it comes in an enormous range of vibrant colors, and is simple to decorate. I am especially partial to gold and silver patterns. They shine like jewels around the Christmas tree, making presents look even more enticing. When clothed in a shining wrap and decorated with festive bows (SEE PAGES 96–97) even the simplest gift takes on a mysterious aura.

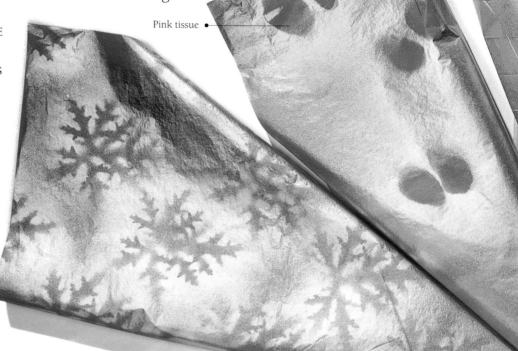

Stencil pattern from Brazil nuts

Pink tissue

STENCILED PATTERNS
Delicate geranium leaves and large Brazil nuts provide the stencils for these patterned papers, although you can use any interestingly shaped forms. Simply place the objects on the paper and spray with gold, silver, or colored paint. Use more than one color if you wish.

TISSUE-PAPER DESIGNS

WHEN YOU SPRAY PAINT tissue paper, place it in a long cardboard box, preferably outdoors.

PLEATED PAPER

1 Pleat a sheet of tissue paper. Place in a long box and spray the silver paint from one side, at an angle, so that paint catches only one edge of the pleats.

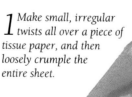

2 When dry, flatten the tissue paper and make another set of pleats at right angles to the first set. Spray paint again.

TIE-DYED EFFECT

1 Make small, irregular twists all over a piece of tissue paper, and then loosely crumple the entire sheet.

2 Apply spray paint lightly and unevenly over the crumpled paper. When it is completely dry, flatten the tissue paper to use.

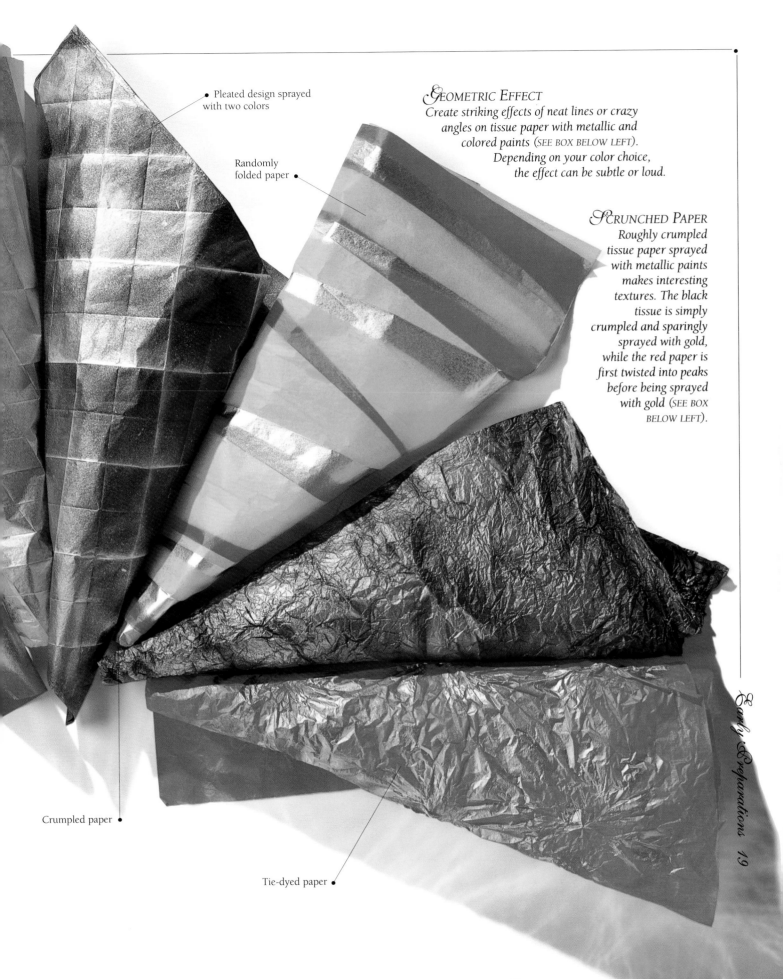

Pleated design sprayed
with two colors

Randomly
folded paper

Crumpled paper

Tie-dyed paper

GEOMETRIC EFFECT

*Create striking effects of neat lines or crazy
angles on tissue paper with metallic and
colored paints (SEE BOX BELOW LEFT).
Depending on your color choice,
the effect can be subtle or loud.*

SCRUNCHED PAPER

*Roughly crumpled
tissue paper sprayed
with metallic paints
makes interesting
textures. The black
tissue is simply
crumpled and sparingly
sprayed with gold,
while the red paper is
first twisted into peaks
before being sprayed
with gold (SEE BOX
BELOW LEFT).*

Early Preparations 19

CHRISTMAS CHAINS

DECORATING THE HOME ADDS TO the excitement of Christmas. The Christmas tree always makes an impact, especially at night when its twinkling lights give the only light in the room. Flower arrangements also bring a room to life, creating both a visual focus and a delicious fragrance. Add to these decorations some original and colorful paper chains, and your rooms will be transformed – not, of course, by magic but by a certain amount of hard work.

It is fun making paper chains because everyone can join in. The garlands and chains shown here are easy to make and can be completed well in advance of Christmas.

STRING OF STARS
Make a chain of metallic green stars, using a template (SEE PAGE 116).

Gold cord

LORDS AND LADIES
The template for this chain (SEE PAGE 116) is cleverly designed to give you a row of alternating female and male figures. If the chain is going to be viewed from both sides, glue two sheets of paper to each other first. Use thin paper, because thick paper can be quite difficult to fold and cut.

Lords and Ladies

FLOWERED GARLAND
Cut twenty-two 4 in (10 cm) squares from tissue paper with pinking shears. Then pleat and crush to give them texture. Straighten and wrap each flower around a 4 ft (1.2 m) length of gold or silver cord. Tie one end tightly with spool wire. Turn the paper back so that the wire tie is inside, and covered by the tissue flower.

JACOB'S LADDER

Contrasting colors of crêpe paper look best in this simple chain. Cut two long strips of crêpe paper, about 1 in (2.5 cm) wide. Glue one end over the other at right angles, then fold the strips back and forth over each other to form accordion-patterned squares. Attach as many chains as you require with glue. Pull out to achieve the ladder effect.

• Crêpe paper

TWISTED LOOPS

This is a simple paper chain made with a twist to catch the light (SEE PAGE 69). Glue two sheets of paper back-to-back so that both sides of the chain links are decorative.

• Gold and silver paper glued back-to-back

Tissue paper •

Exotic Paper Flowers

FLOWERS MADE FROM TISSUE PAPER, thin card stock, and crêpe paper in colors that are as riotous or gentle as you like, look difficult to make but are actually quite simple. I've chosen bright colors for the large flowers, orange-peaches and apricots for the roses, and pastels for the bell flowers, colors that are in keeping with the shapes of the flowers.

Bell Flowers
These flowers look perfect in soft shades. Make them from colored card stock and give them paper-ribbon stamens. Attach a loop of wire or thread to the stamens if you want to hang the flowers.

• Pale pastel card stock

Paper-ribbon stamen •

Jazzy Blooms
Choose brilliantly colored tissue paper to make extravagant peonies, then set them off with a green ruff.

Vibrant tissue • paper

Orange and apricot • crêpe paper

What You Need
Spool wire
Peonies
Three 20 x 15 in (51 x 38 cm) tissue paper
Bell Flowers
5½ x 3 in (14 x 7.5 cm) and 4 x 2½ in (10 x 6.5 cm) thin card stock
1½ x 3½ in (4 x 9 cm) ribbon
Paper glue
Roses
Ten 4 x 3 in (10 x 7.5 cm) crêpe paper

Peach and pink • crêpe paper

• Pinked edge

Hot-pink
and red tissue
paper •

CREPE ROSES

Use the template to cut out
fine inner and five outer petals for each crêpe rose
(SEE PAGE 116). Arrange them in a posy and secure the
narrow ends together with spool wire. They look startling
and effective in brilliant colors, and even better in two
shades. Take your inspiration from real roses or take
them into the realm of fantasy with strange colors,
such as gray and blue or chocolate and lilac.

PAPER BELL FLOWERS & PEONIES

USE PAPER FLOWERS to adorn presents or the
Christmas tree. They last well, so this year's tree
decorations can dress next year's gifts.

PAPER BELL FLOWERS

1 Use the templates from page
116 to make your own
templates for the petals, with
diameters of 2½
in (7 cm) and 2
in (5 cm), and a
3 in (7.5 cm)
stamen, cutting one
end into thin strips.

2 Fold the outer
petals along the
fold lines, gluing the
tab on the inside. Do
the same for the inner petals.

3 Put a drop of
glue on the
base of the inner
petals and stick it
into the outer flower. Roll the
uncut end of the paper ribbon and
glue it into the flower to finish.

TISSUE PAPER PEONY

1 Gather several pieces of colored
tissue together into ½ in (1 cm) wide
pleats, then crumple and twist to form
narrow rolls. Uneven pleating and
crumpling is fine.

2 With pinking shears, cut
several 3 in (7.5 cm)
lengths from the rolls. Make
hanging loops from the wire.

3 Bind the ends of
several rolls with
wire, securing the
loop, and unruffle
the tissue to form the
petals of the flower.

FOREST STILL LIFE

TWIGS, PINE CONES, PAPER RIBBON, moss, and sprigs of fir combine in an inexpensive arrangement that is fun to create. It is easy to put together and, unlike fresh flower arrangements, it does not die within a few days. Woodland plant material makes lovely arrangements. Bark, twigs, boughs, pine cones, and foliage all have strong shapes and because they all grow together naturally, they look absolutely right when combined in the home. The paper ribbon is just rustic enough for the arrangement. A more refined silk ribbon would have been out of place. Dried arrangements look especially effective displayed in glass containers. You might think that the shiny quality of glass would be at odds with rugged plant material. But if you line the vase with moss, wood, bark, leaves, petals, dried mushrooms, or ginger roots, the overall effect is spectacular. Your glossy container enhances rather than detracts from the arrangement.

Orange-red paper ribbon

WHAT YOU NEED
Two 9 x 4½ x 3 in (23 x 11 x 8 cm) bricks dry florist's foam
8 in (20 cm) square glass container
Adhesive clay
Florists' spikes
Blunt knife
3 large handfuls red-dyed lichen
35 woodland twigs, 10 in (25 cm) long
11 ft (3.5 m) paper ribbon
6 giant pine cones
Glue
Straight floral wires
7 sprigs silver fir

METHOD
Cut bricks of dry foam to fit inside the container, leaving a ¾ in (2 cm) gap at the sides. Secure the foam in place with adhesive clay and florists' spikes. Using a blunt knife, wedge clumps of lichen and a few twigs down the sides of the container to hide the foam. With unfurled paper ribbon, firmly tie twigs together in twos and threes to make interesting shapes: some at angles to each other, and others running parallel. Leave the ribbon ends long. Build up an interesting form like this tower, and crown it with a pine cone glued into position. Wire in more cones and then dress the arrangement with silver fir. Spread out the ribbon ends (and cut some back) to finish with a flourish.

INSTANT IMPACT
With its dramatic, angular outline
and the vibrant, contrasting colors
found in the ribbons and foliage,
this dried arrangement has
tremendous visual impact.

Giant pine cone

Woodland twig

HAND-PAINTED CANDLE
I have decorated this apricot
candle with poster paints,
which match the colors of
the arrangement. Water
down the paints to the right
color and then mix with a
couple of drops of dishwashing
liquid – this makes the paint
adhere to the candle.
Paint freehand
or use stencils
to achieve
beautiful
designs.

Silver fir sprig

Red-dyed lichen

Square glass
container

CORNUCOPIA

WALL HANGINGS have much to commend them. Because they sit flat against a wall, they take up little space, yet they can be striking, especially when made in an unusual shape. Think of these almost one-dimensional decorations as paintings that can take many forms – swags, columns, panels, cornucopias, baskets, or even hanging Christmas trees (SEE PAGES 60–61).

A cornucopia is such a symbol of abundance. It just has to be filled to the brim with a profusion of colorful flowers and fruits. You can make your cornucopia, or indeed any of the other wall hangings, from both fresh or dried material. If you use fresh material, you will have to work shortly before the time your decoration is going on display. But if you use dried flowers, seeds, nuts, and fruit, you can complete the arrangement well ahead of Christmas. Store it in a dry place away from the light so that the colors do not fade.

WHAT YOU NEED

Two 28 x 18 in (71 x 46 cm)
chicken wire
Wire cutters
8 handfuls dried moss
Spool wire
70 dried yarrow flowerheads
60 dried red roses
14 dried pink larkspur
12 dried hydrangeas
10 dried Nigella orientalis
seedheads
Straight floral wires
7 gilded pomegranates
3 ft (1 m) paper ribbon
Picture hook

METHOD

Cut the 2 pieces of chicken wire into a horn shape. Tightly sandwich a ½ in (1.5 cm) layer of moss between the pieces of chicken wire and sew the edges together with spool wire. Keep the moss in place by looping pieces of wire through the frame and tying firmly. Either stick the flowers and seedheads directly into the moss, or wire their stems with straight floral wire, then poke into the base. If using lightweight flowers, glue them in position. Push straight floral wire into each pomegranate, through the newspaper stuffing, then wire into position. Make single bows from the paper ribbon (SEE PAGES 96–97) and wire into the arrangement. Wall hangings are surprisingly light: A picture hook holds them in place.

• Red rose

Yarrow flowerhead •

GILDED POMEGRANATES

Enhance the form and color of pomegranates with gold paint and sugar.

1 *Cut a 1½ in (4 cm) hole in the base of the pomegranate and scoop the seeds out with a spoon. Fill the pomegranate with newspaper or dry foam to absorb moisture. Leave in a warm place to dry.*

2 *When dried, spray the top of the pomegranate with gold paint. Lightly sprinkle sugar over the wet paint.*

Gilded
• pomegranate

Pink larkspur

Nigella
orientalis
seedhead

Hydrangea

Salmon-pink
paper ribbon

*Y*EAR-ROUND COLOR
This rich, sunny-colored cornucopia of
flowers and fruit looks pretty hanging on
a wall at any time of year. As the seasons
pass, change the varieties of fruit and
flowers spilling out of it.

POMEGRANATE & PEONY WREATH

THE BEAUTY OF MAKING WREATHS and circlets with dried flowers is that you can prepare them ahead of time and at your leisure. If they do not look too "Christmasy," they can be used to decorate a door or wall for many months. Air-dried larkspur, small-flowered hybrid tea roses, peonies, *helichrysum*, and yarrow, as well as most silica-dried flowers all keep their colors well, as long as they are not put in bright sunlight. I particularly enjoy mixing reds and pinks together; they always make an arrangement look so lively. Adding greenery keeps the flowers looking new and sparkling. I like to use preserved ivy, available from florists' shops. Steeped in glycerine and dye, the leaves appear fresh and keep their strong color indefinitely.

TWIG CIRCLET
A twig circlet decorated with preserved ivy leaves, dried bright yellow helichrysum, *dried red roses, rust- and gold-painted pine cones, and crab apples.*

PRESERVED FLOWERS

MANY-PETALED FLOWERS that are unsuitable for air-drying can be preserved in silica crystals.

1 *Half fill a container that can be sealed with silica crystals. Push a straight floral wire in the base of the flower and place in silica.*

2 *Carefully spoon silica crystals over and between the petals, covering the flower completely. Seal the container. The flower will dry in 2 days.*

WHAT YOU NEED
Green floral tape
12 in (30 cm) diameter foam circle
5 gilded pomegranates
(SEE PAGE 26)
Glue gun
5 handfuls dried moss
Dark green spray paint
4 ft (1.2 m) fabric tubing stuffed with cotton batting
7 wired glycerined and dyed hydrangeas
2 wired dried peonies
10 wired sprays dried pink roses
8 wired sprays dried red roses
20 wired sprigs glycerined and dyed ivy
Fabric loop for hanging

METHOD
Wrap the green floral tape around the foam circle. Indent the foam where you want to place the gilded pomegranates, then glue them into position using a glue gun. Spray-paint the moss dark green. When dry, glue the moss to the wreath to provide a natural-looking base. Wind the fabric tubing around the wreath, then tie it to secure. Wire in the larger flowers. Then insert the smaller ones in curves against the fabric. Wire in the ivy. Attach the fabric loop to the top and back of the wreath for hanging.

Glycerined and dyed
hydrangea

Fruits and Flowers

*Gilded and sugared pomegranates nestle
in sprigs of ivy, dried flowers, and striped
fabric. The vibrantly colored peonies
and roses compete for space with
the pomegranates, creating an
effect of overflowing richness.*

• Peony

• Gilded
pomegranate

Striped fabric •

• Spray of
pink roses

Glycerined and
dyed ivy leaf •

• Spray of red roses

BREAD SCULPTURES

IT IS SAID THAT BREAD always falls on its buttered side. These wondrously decorative breads will never see a speck of butter. Made to hang on the wall, they last for years – or at least until dust gets the best of them. Decorative but inedible breads made from a simple flour, salt, and water recipe are very popular in Scandinavia. They can be made into a variety of shapes, as small decorations for the Christmas tree or larger wall hangings in the forms of baskets, hearts, wreaths, and houses. Alternatively, make an edible sculpture with yeast bread dough – what you gain in texture and flavor is lost in the fine definition of the shapes, however.

• Raffia hanging rope

Whole cloves •

Salt dough • basket

SALT DOUGH
3 cups (340 g) all-purpose flour
1 cup (345 g) salt
4–5 drops vegetable oil
Onion skin and cloves to decorate
Beaten egg white to glaze

Mix flour, salt, and oil; add water to form a stiff dough. Knead until smooth. Form a base for the basket. Roll out a third of the dough to a ¼ in (6 mm) thickness. Cut out a basket shape (keep remaining dough covered). Place on a baking sheet covered with waxed paper. Shape remaining dough into flowers, fruits, and strips for the basket weave and handle. Attach to the base with water. Decorate. Glaze with egg white. Bake at 225° F (110° C) for 8 hours, until it is golden and completely dried out.

HANGING BASKETS
You can make a glazed bread basket of fruits and flowers from either salt dough, that will last for years, or from yeast dough, which can be admired both for its looks and its delicious taste.

YEAST DOUGH

1 package active dried yeast
2 cups (475 ml) lukewarm water
6 cups (680 g) unbleached white
 bread flour
1 tbs salt
Onion skin to decorate
Beaten egg yolk to glaze

Sprinkle the yeast over 4 tablespoons of the lukewarm water. Mix the flour and salt in a large bowl. Pour the dissolved yeast and the rest of the water into the flour and salt, and mix to form a stiff dough. Knead until smooth. Let rise for 1–1½ hours. Punch down. Shape as for the salt dough recipe,

bearing in mind that when the dough rises the appearance will alter slightly. Insert a leather thong for hanging. Place on a baking sheet covered with waxed paper. Let rise for 30 minutes. Glaze the basket with egg yolk. Bake at 350° F (180° C) for 35–45 minutes, until it is a rich, golden brown.

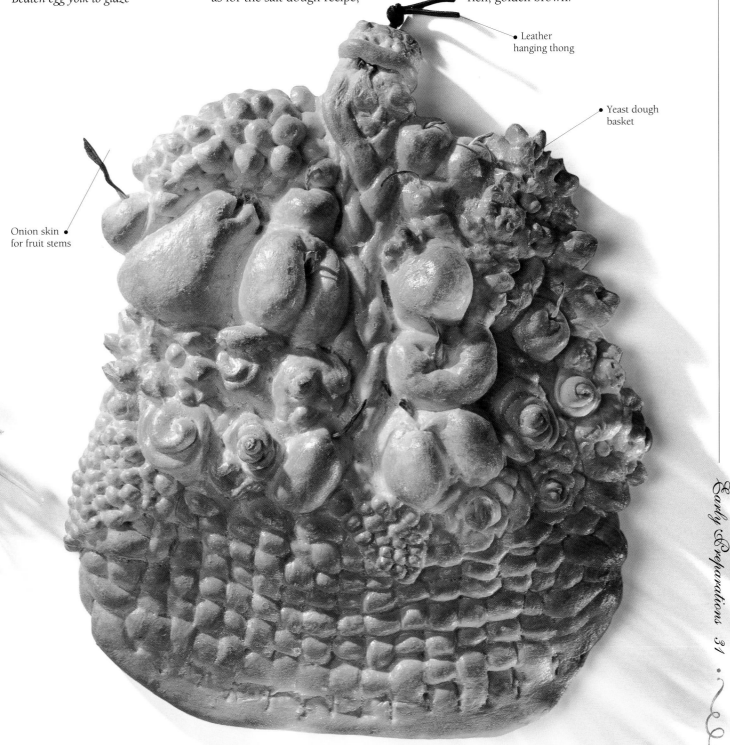

• Leather
hanging thong

• Yeast dough
basket

Onion skin •
for fruit stems

Early Preparations 32

Spice Wreath

MAKE A WREATH THAT IS both fragrant and beautiful. A base of pine, deliciously scented in itself, can last for many months. (Good quality plastic pine garlanding can be incredibly realistic, and will last forever, although you have to forego the fragrance.) Decorate the base with citrus pomanders, little bags made from paper ribbon and filled with crushed spices, and small bundles of lavender and cinnamon sticks. All have such strong scents that the wreath will continue to perfume the air long after the festive season has passed.

WHAT YOU NEED
60 x 6 in (152 x 15 cm) chicken wire
10 handfuls dry moss
20 wired evergreen sprigs
Spool wire
Straight floral wires
Three 2½ in (6 cm) diameter terracotta pots
7 paper-ribbon spice bags
3 lavender bundles
3 cinnamon-stick bundles
7 citrus pomanders
16 sprigs dried hops
Glue
4 decorative seedheads
2 bunches eucalyptus seedheads
7 pine cones
3 sprigs marjoram
10 ft (3 m) paper ribbon

METHOD
Make a moss-filled chicken-wire frame (SEE PAGE 57), inserting wired evergreens to cover, and bend it into a heart shape. Attach straight floral wire to the pots, spice bags, lavender and cinnamon-stick bundles, and pomanders, and secure to the wreath. Fill pots with hops. Glue on seedheads, pine cones, and marjoram. Hang with a paper-ribbon bow.

BUNCH OF HOPS
Tie dried hops and cinnamon sticks together with spool wire, cover with a matching bow, and glue on eucalyptus seedheads to make a simple, scented bunch.

• Pink paper ribbon
• Cinnamon stick
• Dried hops

CITRUS POMANDERS
THESE POMANDERS CONTINUE to release their sharp clove scent for many years.

1 Pierce holes all over the surface of a lime or other small citrus fruit with a skewer. Insert a whole clove into each hole.

2 Put ground orris root in a paper bag. Place the clove-studded lime in the bag, seal, and shake to cover with ground orris root. Store in a warm, dark place for 3 weeks. Remove from the bag and display with a raffia tie.

Paper-ribbon bow

Dried hops

Decorative seedhead

Marjoram

Bag of spices

Eucalyptus seedhead

Lavender bundle

Lime pomander

Cinnamon-stick bundle

SPICY HEART
This fragrant wreath looks perfect hanging in a kitchen or in a hallway where its rich scents will be fully appreciated.

ADVENT WREATH

THE WORD "ADVENT" means an arrival or coming, especially one that is awaited. This event in the Christian year is marked by the four Sundays that precede Christ's birth. In many countries, Advent is celebrated in the home as well as in church with an Advent wreath of evergreen foliage holding five candles. Each Sunday in Advent you light a candle – the fifth and final one is lit on Christmas day. Traditionally, the candles for the four Sundays are red, although the third candle may be pink to match the minister's vestments during that week. The Christmas day candle is white.

To draw attention to the candles, make the wreath with rich, green foliage. Several conifers last amazingly well indoors, keeping both their color and their needles. White fir and Colorado spruce are both excellent. Over the evergreen base, add some dried flowers in shades of red, silver lichen, moss, pine cones, and ribbon.

The Advent wreath looks best on a table, with the white candle placed in the center. For safety, always stay nearby while the candles are lit, and do not allow them to burn too low.

Silver lichen

White fir

Pine cone

Monterey cypress

WHAT YOU NEED

*5 ft x 6 in (152 x 15 cm)
chicken wire
15 handfuls damp moss
15 x 6 in (38 x 15 cm)
chicken wire
Spool wire
Wire cutters
10 sprigs white fir
10 sprigs Monterey cypress
15 dried Helichrysum
10 dried Celosia
18 small pieces dried
silver lichen
12 small pine cones
3 ft (1 m) gold-edged
green ribbon
4 thick pillar candles
1 thick white candle*

METHOD

Make a moss-filled chicken-wire frame (SEE PAGE 57) and bend it into a square. With the smaller piece of chicken wire, make a moss-filled tube and place it diagonally across the square, wiring it in at the corners. Cut a 3 in (8 cm) slit through the frame in each corner and in the center and pull apart to make holes to hold the candles. Insert the foliage into the frame to cover, and decorate with the dried flowers, lichen, pine cones, and ribbon. Finally, add the candles.

Gold-edged green ribbon

Thick pillar candle

CHRISTMAS HERALD
Place this simple Advent wreath on a table beside a window to enjoy it from outdoors as well as indoors. If you use long-lasting foliage, lichen, and dried flowers in rich red shades, this wreath will still look its best on Christmas Day when you light the final, white candle.

Helichrysum

Celosia

Miss Jeffers's Cake

IT WOULD SEEM PARADOXICAL that a rich Christmas cake should feature in the quirky cuisine of tropical Nevis in the West Indies. Miss Jeffers, though, would make this irresistible cake for us when we were staying on the island. The decorations are my addition.

INGREDIENTS
3 lb (1.4 kg) raisins
1½ lb (680 g) currants
1 lb (455 g) prunes
6 oz (170 g) maraschino cherries
12 oz (340 g) candied peel
1½ tsp each ground cinnamon,
    cloves, nutmeg, and salt
1 cup (235 ml) brandy
½ cup (120 ml) rum
2 tbs Madeira
4 tsp vanilla extract
4 oz (115 g) each chopped
    almonds and Brazil nuts
3 cups (680 g) brown sugar
6 sticks (680 g) butter
14 large eggs
6 cups (680 g) all-purpose flour
Juice and rind of 8 limes

METHOD
Mix the fruit, peel, and spices in a large bowl. Sprinkle with alcohol and vanilla extract, cover, and leave for 2 days. Toast nuts and set aside. In a large bowl, beat the sugar and butter until light and fluffy. In another bowl, lightly beat the eggs. Slowly beat the eggs into the butter and sugar. Stir in the flour. Stir in the steeped fruit, lime juice and rind, and nuts. Transfer the mixture to a buttered 12 in (30 cm) baking pan lined with waxed paper. Bake for 6 hours at 275º F (140º C). Store in a sealed container until ready to decorate.

LEAFY RUFF
I always decorate this cake with a ruff of holly and pine (left). In Nevis, Miss Jeffers uses tropical flowers on her cakes.

- Sugared rose petal
- Sugared white grape
- Toasted almond
- Apricot-stuffed prune
- Crystallized ginger
- Toasted pecan
- Toasted Brazil nut
- Sugared kumquat
- Marzipan-stuffed prune
- Crystallized fig
- Crystallized orange peel
- Crystallized cranberry in sliced angelica

FLOWERS, FRUIT, & NUTS

ONE WEEK BEFORE CHRISTMAS, brush this delicious cake with melted apricot jam, and arrange the tantalizing decorations on top.

✃ APRICOT-STUFFED PRUNES ✃

1 *With a small, sharp knife, carefully remove the pits from each of the prunes, keeping the fruit as neat and intact as possible.*

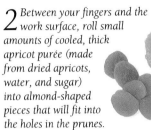

2 *Between your fingers and the work surface, roll small amounts of cooled, thick apricot purée (made from dried apricots, water, and sugar) into almond-shaped pieces that will fit into the holes in the prunes.*

3 *Stuff each prune with an apricot piece. You can also stuff the prunes with marzipan instead of apricot purée.*

✃ SUGARED ROSE PETALS ✃

1 *Gently pull the petals free from a scented well-formed rose with good color.*

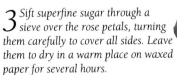

2 *With a small paintbrush, lightly coat each rose petal all over with lightly beaten egg white. Do not saturate the petal.*

3 *Sift superfine sugar through a sieve over the rose petals, turning them carefully to cover all sides. Leave them to dry in a warm place on waxed paper for several hours.*

4 *Re-create the rose, using a piece of crystallized ginger as the centerpiece.*

CRYSTALLIZED FRUIT

HOMEMADE CRYSTALLIZED FRUIT are one of those traditional Christmas delicacies that are just too good to be overlooked in favor of the commercial variety. Although the two-week preparation seems long-winded, the amount of time involved each day is small, and the results are absolutely scrumptious. The homemade versions have much more flavor than store-bought fruit, which I have always found too sweet. Because they last for months in a sealed container, they can be made well ahead of the Christmas rush.

Experiment with all kinds of fruit. Citrus fruits are particularly good. So, too, are tasty plums, apricots, and cherries. Ginger, however, is my all-time favorite, and it also makes an excellent *digestif* after rich food. Crystallized figs and pineapple tend to be rather sweet, but cranberries retain a tang that I find irresistible.

Fig

Prune

Lemon slice

Pink grapefruit segment

Ginger

Whole clementine

Plum

INGREDIENTS

1 1b (450 g) fruit (such as citrus fruits, plums, apricots, cherries, figs, pineapple, cranberries) or cut ginger root, peeled
1¼ cups (295 ml) water
3 cups (680 g) granulated sugar

METHOD

Simmer the fruit or ginger root in the water in a heavy saucepan, until blanched but still firm. Remove the fruit with a slotted spoon and place in a baking dish. Dissolve ¾ cup (170 g) of the sugar in the poaching water. Pour the syrup over the fruit, cover, and leave for 24 hours. On the second day, drain the syrup from the fruit into a saucepan, add ¼ cup (55 g) sugar, and heat until it dissolves. Pour over the fruit, cover, and leave for 24 hours. Repeat for 5 more days. On Day 8, dissolve ⅓ cup (75 g) sugar in the syrup, pour over the fruit, cover, and leave for 2 days. On Day 10, dissolve ⅓ cup (75 g) sugar in the syrup, pour over the fruit, cover, and leave for 4 days. On Day 14, place the fruit on a rack, with waxed paper underneath, and leave to dry in a warm place.

Cranberry

Pineapple slice

Cherry

SWEET, STICKY SPIRAL
A luscious spiral of sweet and tangy crystallized fruit with a dusting of granulated sugar. The sharpest flavors come from the citrus fruits, particularly the segments of pink grapefruit. Cherries and cranberries also retain their strong flavors, as do the small chunks of ginger. Pineapple, figs, and plums are at the sweeter end of the flavor spectrum.

LIQUEUR FRUIT

AS A CHILD, I was wickedly treated to a prune or two that had been preserved in Armagnac at Christmas. I adored them then and still do now. What is so wonderful about liqueur fruit is that the alcohol lends its tantalizing flavor to the fruit and, in turn, the fruit flavors the alcohol, so that each tastes just delicious, yet different from the other. Most ripe, perfect fruit can be preserved in rubber-sealed jars of alcohol that is 25 percent proof or higher or in a mixture of syrup and alcohol. Liqueur fruits should be allowed to mature for at least six weeks. They keep for years. Serve small portions of fruit with some of the liqueur as an after-dinner drink or try it poured over ice cream.

• Muscat Raisins in Liqueur

• Kumquats & Limes in Rum

• Blackberries in Kirsch

BLACKBERRIES IN KIRSCH
1½ lb (680 g) firm, ripe blackberries
2 cups (225 g) red currants
1 cup (225 g) superfine sugar
Red currant leaves, optional
2 cups (475 ml) kirsch

Layer the fruit and sugar in three 1-pt (500-ml) jars, leaving ½ in (1 cm) headroom. Decorate with red currant leaves pushed between the fruit and the glass, if you wish. Pour kirsch over the fruit to cover completely. Tightly seal and leave in a cool, dark place for at least 6 weeks.

KUMQUATS & LIMES IN RUM
4 cups (945 ml) water
1 cup (225 g) superfine sugar
1 lb (455 g) kumquats, pricked
½ lb (230 g) small limes, pricked
7½ cups (1.8 liter) white rum

Bring the water and sugar to a boil, and simmer until the sugar dissolves. Add the fruit and simmer for 5 minutes. Place in two 2-pt (1-liter) jars, leaving ½ in (1 cm) headroom. Reduce the syrup to 1¼ cups (295 ml). Remove from the heat and add the rum. Pour over the fruit. Tightly seal and leave in a cool, dark place for 4 weeks.

MUSCAT RAISINS IN LIQUEUR
1 lb (455 g) muscat raisins
4 cups (945 ml) strong Earl Grey tea
3 cups (710 ml) muscat liqueur

Soak the raisins in the tea overnight. Drain the raisins, and discard the tea. Place the raisins in a 2-pt (1-liter) jar, leaving ½ in (1 cm) headroom. Cover them with muscat liqueur. Seal tightly and leave in a cool, dark place for 8 weeks. Shake the jar gently about once a week.

PRUNES & APPLES IN ARMAGNAC
2 lb (1 kg) large prunes
½ lb (230 g) dried apple rings
6 cups (1.4 liter) apple juice
2 cups (475 ml) Armagnac

Place the prunes, apple rings, and apple juice in a saucepan. Bring to a boil, then remove the saucepan from the heat and leave the fruit to soak overnight. Remove the fruit, discarding the juice, and arrange in two 2-pt (1-liter) jars, leaving ½ in (1 cm) head-room. Pour the Armagnac over the fruit to cover completely. Tightly seal the jars and leave in a cool, dark place for at least 6 weeks.

PEARS & CHERRIES IN PORT
3 cups (710 ml) port
2 cups (455 g) superfine sugar
½ cinnamon stick
5 cloves
3 lb (1.4 kg) firm pears
1 lb (455 g) cherries

Bring the port, sugar, and spices to boil, and stir until the sugar dissolves. Add the fruit and simmer for 20 minutes. Place the fruit in a 2-qt (2.5-liter) jar, leaving ½ in (1 cm) headroom. Boil remaining syrup until reduced to 2 cups (475 ml). Strain, then pour over the fruit to cover. Put on the lid and place the jar in a roasting pan filled with water in a 325° F (150° C) oven for 1 hour to seal. Leave in a cool, dark place for at least 6 weeks.

• Mixed Fruits in Brandy

• Prunes & Apples in Armagnac

• Pears & Cherries in Port

MIXED FRUITS IN BRANDY
5 small white peaches
1 lb (455 g) apricots
10 tangerines, peeled
4 tamarillos, sliced
4 star fruit, sliced
3 kiwi fruit, peeled and sliced
1 miniature pineapple, sliced
  (with peel left on)
3¾ cups (885 ml) water
2 cups (455 g) superfine sugar
Juice of 4 limes
2 vanilla pods
3 cups (710 ml) brandy

Blanch the fruit in boiling water, and remove the peach and apricot skins. Bring the measured water, sugar, lime juice, and vanilla pods to a boil. When the sugar has dissolved, add the fruit, and poach for 6 minutes. Layer the fruit in a 1½-gallon (6-liter) glass jar, leaving ½ in (1 cm) headroom. Add the brandy to the syrup and pour over the fruit to cover. Put on the lid and place the jar in a roasting pan filled with water in a 325° F (150° C) oven for 1 hour to seal. Leave in a cool, dark place for at least 6 weeks.

TRIO OF PUDDINGS

THE TRADITIONAL Christmas pudding is utterly delicious, but many find it far too rich at the end of Christmas dinner. If you love the flavors of Christmas pudding, but would prefer something a fraction lighter, try one of the two other puddings. If you find each one to your taste, make all three!

Ice Cream Pudding •

FROZEN FRUIT
All the flavors of the traditional pudding trapped in a light frozen cream.

• Dried fruit

• White holly leaf

ICE CREAM PUDDING
4 oz (115 g) mixed dried fruit
1 oz (30 g) glacé cherries
1 oz (30 g) candied peel
4 tbs brandy
2 cups (475 ml) heavy cream
⅓ cup (75 g) superfine sugar
1¼ cups (90 g) whole wheat breadcrumbs, finely ground
½ tsp ground cinnamon
⅓ cup (75 g) brown sugar

Mix the fruit and candied peel in a bowl. Sprinkle it with brandy, cover, and leave overnight.

Chop the fruit and peel into small pieces. Beat the cream and sugar until thickened. Freeze until almost set, stirring every half hour.

Meanwhile, combine the breadcrumbs, cinnamon, and brown sugar, then place on a baking sheet. Toast at 400° F (200° C) for 5–10 minutes, until golden and caramelized. Let cool, then break up into small pieces. Stir the soaked fruit and peel, and the caramel pieces into the cream mix. Freeze until solid. Remove 15 minutes before serving. Unmold carefully. Serves 8.

CHRISTMAS BOMBE
3 oz (85 g) mixed dried fruit
½ tsp ground cinnamon
½ tsp ground cloves
½ tsp ground nutmeg
5 tbs rum
3 large eggs plus 2 egg yolks
4 tbs superfine sugar
1¼ cups (295 ml) heavy cream
½ oz (15 g) gelatin
1 large jelly roll

Mix the dried fruit and spices in a bowl. Sprinkle with 2 tbs of the rum, cover, and leave overnight.

Beat the eggs and egg yolks for 5 minutes, until they are thick and foamy. Continue whisking, and slowly whisk in the sugar. Beat for 5 more minutes. Stir in the soaked fruit. Lightly whip the cream, and gently fold it into the fruit mixture. Heat the rest of the rum to just below boiling. Sprinkle the gelatin over the rum, and stir until it has dissolved. Stir the melted gelatin into the fruit mixture. Line a large bowl with ¼ in (5 mm) slices of jelly roll. Spoon the fruit mixture into the cake-lined mold. Cover the fruit mixture with the remaining slices of jelly roll. Cover and refrigerate for several hours before serving. Unmold carefully. Serves 10.

HIDDEN FLAVOR
A Christmas bombe with swirls of sponge hides the lightest mousse, which carries all of the flavors of a Christmas pudding.

• Christmas Bombe

ULTIMATE PUDDING
Luscious fruit, nuts, spices, and a great deal of alcohol make this the ultimate in rich Christmas puddings. Use a round mold for an old-fashioned finish.

• Traditional Christmas Pudding

• Variegated holly

TRADITIONAL CHRISTMAS PUDDING
2 sticks (230 g) unsalted butter
2 tbs molasses
¾ cup (175 ml) brandy
Juice and grated rind of 2 lemons
Grated rind of 2 oranges
4 medium eggs
3¼ cups (230 g) whole wheat breadcrumbs
½ lb (230 g) each currants, sultanas, and
    muscat raisins
1 cup (230 g) dark brown sugar
¾ cup (85 g) whole wheat flour
¾ cup (85 g) almonds, chopped and toasted
¾ cup (85 g) hazelnuts, chopped and toasted
3 oz (85 g) crystallized ginger, chopped
1 large cooking apple, chopped
1 tsp each ground allspice and nutmeg
½ tsp ground cloves

Melt the butter and molasses in a saucepan over low heat. When cool, add the brandy, lemon juice, and lemon and orange rind, then beat in the eggs. Combine the remaining ingredients in a large bowl. Stir the egg mixture into the dry ingredients. Place in a well buttered 2-qt (1 kg) round pudding mold, and steam for 6 hours. Cool for 10 minutes, then remove the mold. Cover the pudding in plastic wrap and store for 2 months. Steam in the mold for a further 1½ hours before serving. Unmold. Serves 16.

Flower & Foliage Ice Bowl

THE INCREDIBLE BEAUTY OF FLOWERS, fruit, berries, and leaves trapped in translucent ice makes an ice bowl one of the most arresting, yet practical Christmas decorations. Serve ice creams, sorbets, fruit salads, or an ice-cold punch in it, or anything that will benefit from the chilling effect of this unusual bowl.

Choose non-toxic plant material that will fit into the ¾ in (2 cm) of ice that forms the bowl. Berries look particularly good and, because the bowl can be made well ahead of Christmas, you can take advantage of the autumn crop of mountain ash, cotoneaster, and viburnum fruits. Roses, freesias, lily petals, ferns, geranium leaves, herbs, and even the humble cabbage can be pressed into use. Slices of limes, tangerines, and kiwi and star fruits also look stunning.

―――――― ✂ ――――――
WHAT YOU NEED
3¼ in (8.5 cm) tall glass jar
6½ x 3½ in (16 x 9 cm)
glass bowl
Matching 8½ x 4½ in
(21 x 11 cm) glass bowl
Clear tape
Non-toxic plant material
Straight floral wire
―――――― ✂ ――――――

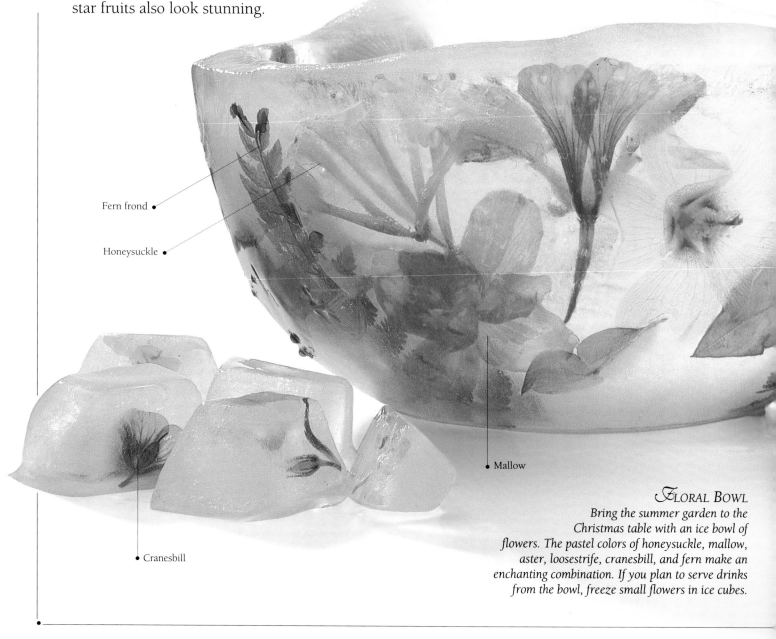

Fern frond •

Honeysuckle •

• Mallow

• Cranesbill

Floral Bowl
Bring the summer garden to the Christmas table with an ice bowl of flowers. The pastel colors of honeysuckle, mallow, aster, loosestrife, cranesbill, and fern make an enchanting combination. If you plan to serve drinks from the bowl, freeze small flowers in ice cubes.

FROZEN COLOR
The glowing colors of the roses and berries and the veining of the cabbage's leaves look luscious suspended in ice. Fill the bowl with kir, a Champagne sorbet, or an exotic fruit salad.

• Loosestrife

Aster •

DECORATIVE ICE BOWLS

IF YOU ARE MAKING AN ICE BOWL for the first time, use fairly bulky plant material such as roses and large leaves. You can easily wedge these in position. Small flowers tend to float to the top, so it is best to make the bowl in different stages by freezing a couple of thin layers.

1 Stack the jar and the bowls. Pour water between the 2 bowls until the water comes to ½ in (1 cm) below the rims. Fill the jar with water to keep the rims level. Hold in place with tape.

2 Select plant material for decorating the ice bowl. I have chosen mountain ash berries, decorative cabbage leaves, miniature amaryllis flowers, sprigs of cypress, and small red roses.

3 Slip the leaves and flowers into the water between the 2 bowls, prodding them into place with straight floral wire. Wedge the larger leaves toward the bases of the bowls and gently squeeze the flowers between the sides. Freeze overnight.

4 Remove the tape and jar, and pour cold water into the smaller bowl. Dip the outer bowl into cold water. (Warm water may cause the ice to crack.) The bowls will gradually come away from the ice. Place on a plate.

Chapter Two

COUNTDOWN TO CHRISTMAS

THE CHRISTMAS SEASON always arrives about two weeks too early for me. School holidays begin at the same time, so you can rely on help from children. Now is the time to make evergreen arrangements and decorate the Christmas tree. Parties abound at this stage, calling for lavish decorations and sumptuous food. Indulge in wickedly rich food without feeling too guilty: chocolate truffles, cookies, and petits fours all look enticing for special occasions.

EVERGREEN ENSEMBLE

Make a long-lasting arrangement in a weathered watering can. The rust hues of the mahonia echo the color of the pepper berries while golden dogwood offsets the tufted pine, gold-striped elaeagnus, and catkin sprays of garrya. Trails of small green dates and privet berries complete the arrangement.

Evergreen Wreaths

THE SIMPLE FRONT DOOR WREATH made from evergreen foliage, twigs, and berries is a most evocative Christmas emblem, dating back to the pagan winter solstice festival. Brilliant red holly berries and rich green winter leaves combine vibrantly, signaling the onslaught of cold weather in northern climates. In the past, whole branches of evergreen were hung above the front door. I have arranged foliage in a fan shape to make a change from the traditional wreath.

Woodland Theme
This evergreen wreath looks best unadorned, so that the natural beauty of the foliage commands all attention. It is most effective on either a simple, rustic front door or a more formal one.

Lichen-covered twig

Skimmia

What You Need
60 x 6 in (152 x 15 cm) chicken wire
10 handfuls damp moss
60 sprigs berried skimmia, wired
50 lichen-covered twigs
50 stems berried holly, leaves removed
Spool wire

Method
Prepare a moss-filled chicken-wire frame (SEE PAGE 57), wiring skimmia sprigs into the front of the frame. Next, stick lichen-covered twigs and short pieces of holly into the frame, keeping them flowing in the same direction as the skimmia. Let the plant material extend about 4 in (10 cm) beyond the frame's outer edge, but only 2–3 in (5–7.5 cm) over the inner edge. Wire the 2 ends of the wreath together.

Weatherproof
red ribbon

Silver fir

Berried holly
with leaves removed

DOOR DECORATION
*Extremely long-lasting, this hanging
bunch of conifer and holly needs only
a minimum of added decoration, in the
form of simple red bows. Its strong
shape is particularly suited to a
large front door.*

WHAT YOU NEED

*3 large silver fir branches
5 stems berried holly,
leaves removed
3 small silver fir branches
Spool wire
12 ft (4 m) weatherproof
red ribbon*

METHOD

On a flat surface, lay the
large fir branches in a fan shape. Overlap the cut
ends by about 2 in (5 cm). Arrange the holly on
top. Fill in any gaps with the smaller pieces of fir.
Tie the bunch firmly together with spool wire.
Attach a hanging loop of wire or ribbon to the
back at the top. Cover with a bow and tie small
bows (SEE PAGES 96–97) among the branches.

Wreaths from Heaven

THE FRONT DOOR WREATH is the most welcoming of all Christmas arrangements. Simple but strong color themes work best for either minimal evergreen wreaths made from holly, pine, and fir, or for "over-the-top" glittery creations like these vibrant gold and silver designs.

When making door wreaths, remember that they must be strong enough to withstand the wind and weather for about three weeks, not to mention the constant opening and closing of the front door. To keep the foliage fresh, stuff the chicken wire with damp moss. This makes a strong base for attaching both the foliage and any decorations.

Glowing Gold
Cherubs reach to catch the stars in this extravagant gold arrangement. The ribbon spiraling around the wreath echoes the curved shapes of the cherubs, creating a sparkling and lively decoration for your front door.

Golden, glittered lotus seedhead •

Silvered star

Silvered cherub

Variegated holly

• Miniature wrapped present

Gilt Brazil nut •

Silver Variation
The same cherubs and stars, this time sprayed and glittered with silver, give the wreath a frosty look. Variegated holly and miniature wrapped packages add color to the bottom half, while touches of red from the berries and ribbons introduce spots of warmth here and there.

What You Need
60 x 6 in (152 x 15 cm) chicken wire
10 handfuls damp moss
20 sprigs wired, long-lasting conifer
Spool wire
Glue gun
Straight floral wires
2 cherubs and 3 stars, sprayed gold
6 lotus seedheads, sprayed gold and glittered
7 Brazil nuts, sprayed gold
7 brass ornaments
6½ ft (2 m) gold ribbon

Method
Make a circular moss-filled chicken wire frame (SEE PAGE 57), sticking wired conifer sprigs into the frame to cover. Glue straight floral wires to the backs of the cherubs and stars, then stick them into the frame. Wire the seedheads, nuts (SEE PAGE 61), and ornaments into position. Loosely wrap gold ribbon around the wreath. Make matching bows (SEE PAGES 96–97) and attach.

Gilt star

Gold
ribbon

Douglas fir

Brass
ornament

Gilt cherub

FLAMBOYANT FLOWERS

A LARGE FLOWER ARRANGEMENT has greater impact than a number of small ones. Display a large vase prominently, and then arrange tiny vases with just a few of the flowers used in the main display around the rest of the house. Choose flowers with strong shapes that look good in silhouette, and stems and foliage with interesting forms. Here, cyclamen grow in their own pots, alongside cut holly, lilies, roses, euphorbia, ranunculus, strelitzia, and powerfully shaped gourds, with gold candles adding the dimension of light. They are arranged in an antique copper container.

Picotee cyclamen

Deep pink rose

WHAT YOU NEED
Large oval copper container
1 plastic garbage bag
2 cyclamen plants
Six 9 x 4½ x 3 in (23 x 11 x 8 cm) bricks wet florist's foam
4 gold candles
7 stems Euphorbia fulgens
7 stems berried holly, leaves removed
7 roses
5 stems Euphorbia seguieriana
5 gloriosa lilies
5 ranunculus
5 strelitzia flowers
3 strelitzia leaves
3 gourds

Euphorbia seguieriana

METHOD
Line the container with the plastic garbage bag, and position the plants. If necessary, use foam to raise them. Soak the other blocks of foam and fill the container, wedging them securely in place. Position the candles in the foam. Add more foam if extra height is needed. Arrange the plant material so that it spills lavishly out of the container. Leave space around the candles, so that there is no risk of the display catching fire.

Gourd

Berried holly

Strelitzia leaf

GLOWING COLOR
A weathered copper container
bursting with brash color –
golden orange, military red,
and crushed pink – makes a
dramatic display for a hall
table or sideboard.

Euphorbia
fulgens

Strelitzia flower

Copper
container

Gloriosa lily

BELL & ORB

HANG THESE EVERGREEN Christmas spheres in a porch or hallway where they can be seen to best advantage during the festive season. If you use damp florist's foam as a base, they will look fresh for at least two weeks. They will last even longer if you hang them outside. A traditional holly sphere is easy to make. The bell is only a little more complicated. I like to use berried holly by itself because it looks so rich. Mistletoe, however, looks rather sparse on its own, so I mix it with other foliage such as boxwood, yew, and juniper. Tangerines add cheerful color.

Holly Bell
WHAT YOU NEED
12 x 7 x 7 in (30 x 18
x 18 cm) brick wet
florist's foam, soaked
26 x 12 in (65 x 30 cm)
chicken wire
Spool wire
120 sprigs berried
holly
13 ft (4 m)
green ribbon

METHOD
Cut the florist's foam to make
a cone 12 in (30 cm) high, and
7 in (18 cm) wide at the base,
tapering to 2 in (5 cm) at the top.
Cover it with chicken wire and secure with spool
wire. Tie several lengths of spool wire to the top of
the cone for extra strength. Hang it at eye level, so
you can work on it easily. Push short sprigs of
berried holly into the top of the frame and long
sprigs at the base, to accentuate the bell shape.
Attach a bow at the top and base (SEE PAGES 96–97),
and twist matching ribbon around the hanging wire.

• Variegated
holly with
berries

• Gilt-edged
green ribbon
with gold stars

Tangerine

Mistletoe

Fruiting
ivy

Gilt-edged
white ribbon
with gold stars

Mistletoe Orb
WHAT YOU NEED
6 in (15 cm) square wet
florist's foam, soaked
20 x 12 in (50 x 30 cm)
chicken wire
Spool wire
3 lb (1.5 kg) mistletoe
40 sprigs flowering ivy
18 tangerines, wired
(SEE PAGE 61)
10 ft (3 m) white ribbon

METHOD
Push the corners of the foam in to make a
rough sphere. Cover with the chicken
wire and secure with spool wire. Attach
several lengths of spool wire to the top of
the sphere for extra strength and hang, so
you can work on it easily. Stick sprigs
of mistletoe and ivy into the foam to
completely cover. Wire in the tangerines.
Decorate with a bow at the bottom (SEE
PAGES 96–97), and twist matching ribbon
around the hanging wire.

FIR LANTERN

TO GIVE YOUR HOME a wonderfully old-fashioned feel, make an evergreen lantern lit with glowing candles. As with the traditional lanterns made in Victorian times, hang it in a window, to be enjoyed from both outside and inside the house. Alternatively, suspend it in a hall or on a stairway, where it can be viewed from all angles. As the candles burn down, their flames get closer to the foliage: to reduce the risk of fire, be present while the lantern is lighted.

Sturdy chain •

• Miniature package

Small pine cone •

GLOWING EVERGREENS
A simple green lantern
constructed from rings of
fir and four long-lasting
candles. To make a larger
lantern that can hold more
candles, use bigger rings and add
one more vertical ring for stability.

• Metallic red
ribbon

• Long-lasting candle

― ✁ ―

WHAT YOU NEED

Two 60 x 6 in (152 x 15 cm)
chicken wire
One 63 x 6 in (160 x 15 cm)
chicken wire
30 handfuls damp
sphagnum moss
60 sprigs long-lasting conifer,
such as white fir, yew, or thuja
Spool wire
10 ft (3 m) ribbon
Sturdy chain
4 pronged candle holders
4 candles
36 small decorations such as
pine cones and miniature
wrapped packages, wired

― ✁ ―

METHOD

Make 3 moss frames,
one larger than the
others (SEE RIGHT).
Wrap ribbon around
each. Holding the 2
small rings vertically,
push one through the other
to form a sphere. Bind tightly with
spool wire. Holding the larger ring
horizontally, slip it over the small rings
to complete your sphere. Bind firmly.
Wire a sturdy chain to the top of the
sphere for hanging. Stick the candle
holders into the horizontal ring and check that they are
secure. Finally, wire in the decorations and add the candles.

CHICKEN-WIRE FRAME

CHICKEN-WIRE FRAMES filled with moss make strong,
adjustable bases for many of my wreaths. Larger
pieces of chicken wire can also be cut, filled with
moss, and stitched together for solid shapes
(SEE PAGES 26–27 AND 60–61).

1 *Lay the chicken wire*
flat. Arrange most of the
sphagnum moss in a straight row
down the length of the chicken wire.

2 *Starting at one end, bend*
the chicken wire around the moss
to form a 1 in (2.5 cm) diameter roll,
adding more moss if necessary to make a solid filling.

3 *Bend the roll into a circle and cover with foliage, either by*
securing overlapping sprays in place with spool wire, or by
inserting wired evergreens (sprigs with straight floral wire
wound tightly around each
stem) into the frame.
Attach the ends
with wire.

Countdown to Christmas 57

Silk Flower Garland

GARLANDS LEND A TRADITIONALLY festive air to the home, trailing around a doorway, window, or fireplace, or twisting up a banister. Preparing a garland can take a great deal of time, but because this one is made from dried material and silk flowers you can construct it well in advance. After Christmas, if you take the garland down carefully and store it in a box in a dark, dry place, it will last for several seasons. A threaded garland like this one looks equally good when viewed from all sides.

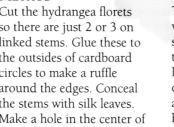

WHAT YOU NEED
25 silk hydrangea
flower heads
Glue
Forty 1 in (2.5 cm)
cardboard circles
Large-eyed darning needle
12 ft (4 m) green garden twine
1 matchstick
3 lb (1.5 kg) large, round,
dried leaves such as silver
dollar eucalyptus

METHOD
Cut the hydrangea florets so there are just 2 or 3 on linked stems. Glue these to the outsides of cardboard circles to make a ruffle around the edges. Conceal the stems with silk leaves. Make a hole in the center of each piece of cardboard.

Thread the darning needle with twine and tie a matchstick on the other end. Push the needle through 10 dried leaves at a time, pulling them down to the end of the twine, and intermittently adding a hydrangea circle. Repeat until the garland is complete.

EXOTIC RUFFLES

*The soft, muted colors of the
hydrangea flowers and the ruffled
edges of the dried leaves complement
each other well, making an unusual
but sophisticated, festive decoration.
You could use other silk flowers
in different colors for the
garland, but the size and
shape of the hydrangeas
is particularly suitable.*

Round dried leaf ●

Silk hydrangea flower ●

FRUIT & NUT TREE

TRADITIONAL SWAGS OR FESTOONS are essentially thick ropes of plant material and decorations that you can hang on a wall, drape around the mantelpiece, or use to adorn windows, doorways, and arches. Hanging panels are similar, but more fun, because you can make them into any shape: a column, a basket, an oversized bow, a cornucopia (SEE PAGES 26–27), or a hanging tree. This tree panel hangs fairly flat against the wall, yet it is a good size, making it ideal for a room with no space for a traditional tree. Composed of silver fir, red apples, limes, and gilded walnuts, it will last for several weeks without flagging.

OTHER COLORS
For a different color scheme, use tangerines or small oranges, gilded pomegranates (SEE PAGE 26), pinkish red lychees, and gilded Brazil or pecan nuts, all of which stay fresh throughout the festive season.

WHAT YOU NEED
Two 1½ x ¾ x 45 in (7 x 2 x 112 cm) wood slats
1½ x ¾ x 36 in (7 x 2 x 90 cm) wood slat
chicken wire
Spool wire
12 ft x 12 in (4 m x 30 cm)
Large bag damp moss
100 sprigs wired, silver fir
1 strand white lights
20 wired red apples
15 wired limes
60 wired and gilded walnuts
Piece of bark
Strong hook

METHOD
Nail the wood slats together to form a triangle. Tightly stretch chicken wire over one side of the frame. Secure with spool wire. Place a thick layer of moss on the frame side of the chicken wire. Stretch and secure the remaining chicken wire over the moss, to sandwich it.

Sew loops of spool wire through the frame to hold the moss firm. Push the fir into one side of the frame to cover. Attach the lights across the back, poking the bulbs through to the front. Decorate with the wired fruit and nuts. Attach the bark to the base with spool wire.

Secure a hanging loop of spool wire to the top and suspend from a strong hook.

WIRING FRUIT

*B*end a hook in one end of a straight floral wire. Poke the straight end through the base of the fruit and pull it through until the hook pierces the fruit and holds firm. The wire is not strong enough to hold the fruit unsupported, but when it is pulled and looped back through an arrangement, it should easily hold.

WIRING TECHNIQUES

WIRE NUTS AND FRUIT so that you can fasten them easily in place on your arrangement.

WIRING & GILDING NUTS

*B*end one end of a straight floral wire into a zig zag. Attach the bent end to a nut using fast-drying glue. When the glue is dry, spray the nut with gold paint. For a "distressed" effect, lightly spray a rich red over the gold, making sure some of the gold still shows through.

WOODLAND SWAG

FOR CENTURIES, THE PEOPLE in northern climates have brought branches of evergreen foliage into the home for the Christmas season. To me, simple garlands and swags made with several types of evergreens are as beautiful as any Christmas decoration. Garlands lend your rooms their delicious fragrance: sharp, tangy, and sometimes citruslike. Furthermore, they do not need glitter, ornaments, or bows to add to their intrinsic, but subtle, beauty.

Silver fir

Glycerined and dyed copper beech

Dried mushroom

Bottlebrush

SHADES OF GREEN

Long-lasting silver fir and golden cypress form the
predominant foliage, adding blue and gold tints to the green.
The glycerined and dyed copper beech introduces a glimmer
of deep red. Bottlebrush leaves form delicate spikes
among the conifer foliage, and large, dried, flat
mushrooms and pine cones, which both have
wonderful shapes, give varying textures.

Golden cypress •

Pine cone •

Fruiting ivy •

WHAT YOU NEED
8 ft x 6 in (2.4 m x 15 cm)
chicken wire
15 handfuls damp or
dry moss
30 sprigs wired, glycerined
and dyed copper beech,
silver fir, bottlebrush,
fruiting ivy, and
golden cypress
20 pine cones
15 dried mushrooms
Straight floral wires

METHOD
Make a moss-filled chicken-wire
frame (SEE PAGE 57, STEPS 1 AND 2).
Ideally, you should use damp
moss, unless you intend to hang
the swag against matte paint or
wallpaper. Bend the frame into
a swag shape. Stick overlapping
sprigs of wired foliage into the
swag. Do the 2 sides first, starting
at the bases. For the central part of the
swag, work from the middle outward.
Wire the pine cones and mushrooms
with straight floral wire, and attach.

LANTERNS

A SOFTLY shining lantern in the window is a welcoming sight at Christmas. Its friendly glow creates a magical atmosphere, especially when placed alongside more traditional decorations. Try hanging a lantern in a corner of a room, or group two or three star and moon lanterns together in a window. They can be lit by small 40-watt bulbs held in normal light sockets, and hung from the lighting wire. Because these lanterns are made of paper, they are quite delicate and only should be used indoors.

• Lichen-covered branch

• Handmade textured paper

• Moon lantern

• Star lantern

SUN LANTERN
Make a three-dimensional rectangular frame, securing the garden stakes with glue. Glue a rectangle of textured paper around the frame. Cut out 4 suns from the same paper, and color them orange. Glue to the inside of the lantern. Finish the top and bottom edges with thin strips of the same paper. Glue a piece of cord diagonally between 2 of the top corners, and attach to the lighting wire to hang.

STAR & MOON
Cut 2 moons or 2 stars from textured paper. Glue the edges together. In the back, cut a square hole, 2½ in (6 cm) across, for the bulb and socket. Glue straight floral wires across the back of the lantern, from edge to edge. When the glue is dry, slightly bend the wires out into arcs to give the lantern dimension. Insert the light and hang.

JAPANESE LANTERN

Make 2 squares, one from the short and one from the long garden stakes. Glue the smaller frame into the larger frame to form a diamond inside a square when viewed from above. Glue long sheets of paper to the smaller frame, and shorter ones to the larger frame. Tie cord diagonally between 2 corners. Attach to the light.

PYRAMIDAL LANTERN

Glue the stakes together to form a pyramidal frame. Glue a triangle of paper around the frame, leaving the top open. Insert the light. Tie cord at the top to secure.

• Hanging cord

• Wooden lantern frame

WHAT YOU NEED

Glue
Handmade textured paper
Light fixture with 40-watt bulb
Gold cord
Sun Lantern
Eight 5 in (13 cm) garden stakes
Four 9 in (23 cm) garden stakes
Orange ink
Star & Moon Lanterns
Straight floral wires
Pyramidal Lantern
Six 9 in (23 cm) garden stakes
Japanese Lantern
Four 7 in (18 cm) garden stakes
Four 11 in (28 cm) garden stakes

TRADITIONAL TREE

RED AND GREEN ARE the traditional colors of Christmas. Wonderfully vibrant when combined, they each seem to make the other richer, deeper, and more lustrous. Several weeks before the festive season starts, the stores are piled high with red and green decorations. You can make your own Christmas stars, painted spheres, cranberry decorations, and fabric eggs, or have a mixture of home-made and store-bought to deck the tree for a special, traditional Christmas.

CHRISTMAS STARS
Cut out stars from thick cardboard or balsa wood. Paint red and green designs on both sides, and attach a loop for hanging.

PAINTED SPHERES
Make your own hand-painted ornaments. Attach thread loops to table tennis balls before you paint them.

CRANBERRY SWAGS
Thread firm cranberries onto long lengths of thread, knotted at the end.

WHAT YOU NEED
For a 6 ft (1.8 m) tree:
16 in (41 cm) diameter terracotta pot
2 strands red candle-shaped, clip-on lights
40 wrapped Christmas eggs
20 cranberry spheres
20 Christmas stars
20 yds (18 m) cranberry swags
18 dried rose posies
15 painted spheres

FABRIC EGGS
Cover blown eggs with rich fabrics.

RUBY-RED SPHERES
A richly colored sphere of berries adds its distinctive color to the tree.

DRIED ROSE POSIES

Small bunches of dried roses and preserved ivy leaves secured with bows make unusual tree decorations (SEE PAGE 71).

RICH RED DECORATIONS

TIME IS INVARIABLY SHORT around Christmas, so make the wrapped Christmas eggs well ahead, and store until needed. The cranberry spheres, however, need to be made about one week before Christmas.

WRAPPED CHRISTMAS EGGS

1 Cut out a square of raw silk, large enough to draw around a blown egg. Gather one side of the square and tie with red thread, leaving ends to make a hanging loop.

2 Place the egg on the silk, with the narrow part at the gathered end. Stitch up the open side of the little fabric bag.

3 Gather the fabric at the top of the egg, and finish by tying a bow with gold cord.

CRANBERRY SPHERES

1 Bend one end of a straight floral wire, for the hook. Insert the straight end into a ¾ in (1.5 cm) foam ball. Pull through, threading a hanging loop under the hook. Pull tight. Cut off the other end, leaving ¾ in (2 cm) to bend into the foam.

2 Glue cranberries onto the ball, positioning them as closely together as possible to leave no gaps. These cranberry spheres last about 2 weeks.

Silver Tree

CHOOSE A DESIGN THEME for your Christmas tree, using just one or two colors. Silver, reminiscent of frost, ice, and snow, makes the tree shimmer with cold. Tiny points of red accentuate the chill.

What You Need

For a 6 ft (1.8 m) tree:
- 20 in (51 cm) square tub
- 2 strands white lights
- 45 iridescent icicles
- 20 miniature presents
- 20 silver stars
- 20 red berries
- 15 glittering glass balls
- 12 silvered pine cones
- 12 silver glass cones
- 12 silver bows
- 10 yd (9 m) paper chains
- 10 white spheres

Tiny Gifts
Cover little boxes with silver paper and add trimmings.

Painted Cones
Pine cones are a beautiful shape and a natural choice for decorating fir trees.

White Spheres
Spheres come in all colors. These snowballs are decorated with sprigs of holly.

Iridescent Icicles
The long, pointed shapes of these realistic glass icicles give the tree strong definition.

Stars
Paint egg white onto glass stars, and sprinkle with glitter to create a frosted effect.

Silver Bows
Tie wire-edged silver ribbon into extravagant, eye-catching bows (SEE PAGES 96–97).

Glittering Glass Balls
Clear glass balls, patterned with a tracery of shimmering silver, glisten with reflections from the tree lights.

Glass Cones
The early Victorians decorated their trees with beautiful glass balls. These cones are based on a traditional design.

TWISTED CHAINS
Metallic paper chains twirled around the tree catch the light on their many facets.

RED BERRIES
Twist artificial wired berries to the tree to add drops of fiery red.

SILVER DECORATIONS

WHILE YOU CAN BUY A HOST OF silver decorations from the shops, it is fun to make some of the easier ones, such as the paper chains and silvered pine cones, yourself.

⫷ PAPER CHAINS ⫸

1 Choose 2 different sheets of silver wrapping paper and glue them back to back, so that the attractive sides show. Cut the paper into ¾ in (2 cm) strips.

2 Attach a piece of double-sided sticky tape to one end of each paper strip. Make a loop with a single twist in it. Thread each through the previous loop to make a chain.

⫷ SILVERED PINE CONES ⫸

1 Bend a straight floral wire around the pine cone near its base, leaving one end long enough for securing the cone to the tree.

2 Twist the wire tightly around the cone to secure. Spray the cone with silver paint. While the paint is still wet, sprinkle with silver glitter. Do this job outdoors, preferably spraying into an old box.

DRIED FLOWER TREE

DRIED FLOWERS COMBINE TO make a surprisingly colorful tree. The paper bows enhance and strengthen the shades of the flowers while strands of matching raffia drift in a spiral up the tree, creating a swirl of movement.

SPRAY OF SCARLET ROSES
Red and green are opposing colors, so you will find that the impact of the little scarlet roses is strengthened by the backdrop of rich, dark green leaves. Pink heightens the drama.

COLORED RAFFIA
Color raffia with spray paints. Do this outside on a still day. Place 30–40 strands of raffia in a large old box. Spray into the box, turning the strands so that they are colored all over. Pull the raffia through the tree, allowing strands to catch on the branches.

OPULENT PEONY
A single large pink peony nestling among dark leaves makes a striking decoration. If the peony looks a little droopy, revive it with a burst of steam from a kettle, and blow it back into shape.

MOODY LARKSPURS
Deep mauve-blue larkspurs tied with a lilac ribbon strongly contrast with the other dried flowers on the tree.

HEADY HYDRANGEAS
These deep plum-red hydrangeas, preserved in glycerine to which dye has been added, are tied together with glycerined ivy leaves and a lilac bow.

SUMMER ROSES
I have combined these yellow roses (still vibrant with summer color) with ivy leaves, and introduced contrast with a blue-pink paper bow.

DRIED ROSES
Pink roses and a red bow work together wonderfully, each making the other more intense.

CAMPION
Dried pink campion retains a fresh look. A pale aqua bow accents the color.

AIR-DRIED FLOWERS

1 Choose flowers with firm, well-shaped flowerheads for air-drying. Remove any leaves and flowers from the ends of the stems.

2 Tie 5 or 6 of the flowers together and hang in a cool dark place until dry.

WHAT YOU NEED
For a 6 ft (1.8 m) tree:
18 in (46 cm) square fiberglass container
2 strands colored lights
60 dried posy decorations
Five 4 ft (1.2 m) bundles colored raffia

DRIED FLOWER DECORATIONS

BUNDLES OF DRIED FLOWERS and ivy leaves are simple to arrange. Make the bows in several colors of paper ribbon and tie them to the flower bunches. Use the binding wire to hang them from the Christmas tree.

DRIED POSY DECORATIONS

1 Gather a few dried flowers of your choice. Here I have used helichrysum. Add a few glycerined ivy leaves and arrange in a small posy.

2 Place a straight floral wire under the posy. Bend down a short end of wire to run parallel with the stems. Tightly twist the rest of the wire around the stems, just below the leaves to make the binding extra secure.

3 Make a single bow out of paper ribbon (SEE PAGES 96–97). Tie the bow onto the posy with a thin piece of the same ribbon.

MEXICAN TREE

MEXICO IS A COUNTRY of vibrant, shocking colors – the hottest reds, the most vicious pinks, vivid yellows and golds, and jewel-like greens and blues. Cover your tree with these clashing colors to add Latin heat to the home at Christmas.

DAZZLING HEARTS
Choose the brightest metallic wrapping papers you can find for making paper hearts. Combine red with pink, violet with orange, and green with blue to achieve a riotous color scheme.

FLASHY SPHERES
Lightweight and inexpensive, tissue balls are simple to make. They are also showy with their mixed frills of the brightest colors.

RED-HOT CHAINS
Wear rubber gloves to string chilies because the juice stings. The effort is well worth it, for they look enchanting among the branches.

TIN DECORATIONS
Search the stores for shiny Mexican decorations made of painted tin cut into shapes of butterflies, birds, roosters and chickens, fish, fruit, moons, stars, and suns. They are surprisingly inexpensive.

TINSEL TUFTS
Cut ½ in (1 cm) tufts of tinsel garland. Perch tufts on the ends of branches to glitter like little mirrors as they reflect the Christmas tree lights.

WHAT YOU NEED
For a 6 ft (1.8 m) tree:
15 in (38 cm) diameter
terracotta pot
2 strands white lights
8 yd (7 m) chili chain
35 tin decorations
25 tissue balls
15 paper hearts
3 ft (1 m) tinsel garland

MEXICAN PAPER DECORATIONS

TISSUE PAPERS AND SHINY metallic wrapping papers are available in a great range of designs. Make decorations in the brightest colors to convey a Mexican theme.

TISSUE BALLS

1 Place three 20 x 15 in (51 x 38 cm) rectangles of tissue paper on top of each other. Roughly pleat them, gathering the paper with the thumb and 2 fingers of each hand. Repeat with 3 more pieces of tissue paper.

2 Twist and scrunch the pleated papers. Pull them straight, and cut into 5 in (13 cm) lengths with scissors or pinking shears.

3 Take 5 lengths, and tie them around the middle with wire or thread. Make a loop for hanging. Separate and fluff the layers of tissue paper apart to form a ball.

PAPER HEARTS

1 Use the template on page 116 to cut out 2 shapes from metallic paper. Fold each in half. Make 2 or more cuts, from the folded edge to the start of the curved section.

2 Weave the strips of the 2 shapes together to form a checkered pattern.

3 Use a hole puncher to make a hole just below the "V" of the heart, and attach a loop of cord or ribbon for hanging.

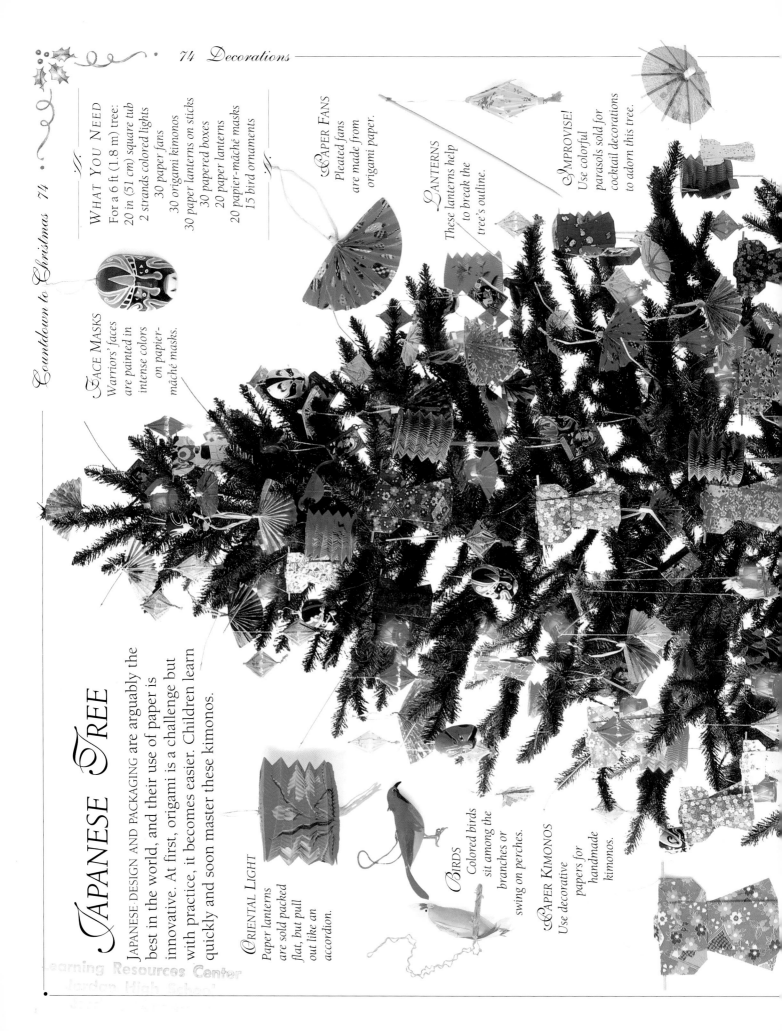

JAPANESE TREE

JAPANESE DESIGN AND PACKAGING are arguably the best in the world, and their use of paper is innovative. At first, origami is a challenge but with practice, it becomes easier. Children learn quickly and soon master these kimonos.

ORIENTAL LIGHT
Paper lanterns are sold packed flat, but pull out like an accordion.

BIRDS
Colored birds sit among the branches or swing on perches.

PAPER KIMONOS
Use decorative papers for handmade kimonos.

WHAT YOU NEED
For a 6 ft (1.8 m) tree:
20 in (51 cm) square tub
2 strands colored lights
30 paper fans
30 origami kimonos
30 paper lanterns on sticks
30 papered boxes
20 paper lanterns
20 papier-mâché masks
15 bird ornaments

FACE MASKS
Warriors' faces are painted in intense colors on papier-mâché masks.

PAPER FANS
Pleated fans are made from origami paper.

LANTERNS
These lanterns help to break the tree's outline.

IMPROVISE!
Use colorful parasols sold for cocktail decorations to adorn this tree.

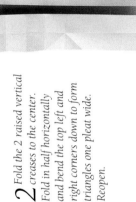

TAPERED BOXES
Cover matchboxes with Japanese paper to emphasize the Japanese theme.

ORIGAMI KIMONOS

1 Fold a 9 in (23 cm) square of origami paper in half vertically. Unfold. Pleat vertically into 8 as shown. Unfold. Pleat the top half horizontally into 4, as shown. Unfold.

2 Fold the 2 raised vertical creases to the center. Fold in half horizontally and bend the top left and right corners down to form triangles one pleat wide. Reopen.

3 Turn the sheet over and form a small diamond by pushing in the top 2 corners of the raised section, and fold down as shown.

4 Turn the paper over and bend the top pleat down. Lift the top of the diamond up from the back, and pleat the central horizontal fold up. Fold the outer vertical edges into the center; the triangles from step 2 will bend into place.

5 Pleat the top half of the diamond, as shown, to form the collar. Fold back the outer vertical pleats of the lower half of the kimono at an angle to form the skirt. Next, fold in the bottom corners of the kimono sleeves.

6 Turn over and press flat with a hot iron. Insert a trimmed bamboo skewer through the sleeves, and glue down the paper to secure. Wire the bamboo skewer ends for hanging.

Countdown to Christmas 76

LEMON COOKIES

You can create a multitude of varying patterns with just two or three different colors.

WHAT YOU NEED

For a 6 ft (1.8 m) tree:
17 in (43 cm) square terracotta pot
2 strands colored lights
30 cellophane bags of sweets
Five 4 ft (1.2 m) popcorn strands
10 gold-wrapped marrons glacés
40 painted lemon cookies
15 gold and silver cookies
15 gingerbread people
20 candy canes

GINGERBREAD

Use silver and gold sugar balls to suggest mouths, eyes, shoes, buttons, and gloves. Vary the designs to create individual personalities.

GINGERBREAD TREE

HALF THE FUN OF THIS CHRISTMAS TREE comes from preparing the decorations. Everyone can help to make and paint the cookies, and cover the sweets in cellophane. The only trouble with this tree is that it may not stay dressed for too long!

JELLYBEAN BAGS

Bundle up jellybeans or chocolates in cellophane, gathered with gold cord. Finish with a bow.

POPCORN STRANDS

Thread popcorn onto 4 ft (1.2 m) lengths of thread, and drape around the tree.

CANDY CANES
You can either hook these pretty twirled candy canes over the branches or hang them from gold cord.

PAINTED COOKIES

1 Paint the unbaked lemon cookies with egg-yolk glazes in a variety of colors (SEE PAGE 80).

2 After the cookie is baked, it will have a shiny, translucent glaze. When cool and hard, thread a loop of ribbon or cord through the hole.

EDIBLE ADORNMENTS

BAKE THE COOKIES to well done to keep them from crumbling. Make hanging holes before baking. The holes must be large enough to thread through a piece of ribbon or cord.

GINGERBREAD PEOPLE

1 Make a cone with a very pointed end from a rectangular piece of waxed paper. Tape to secure. Fill it with icing made from confectioners' sugar and water. Tear or cut a tiny hole across the tip for drawing.

2 Squeeze the cone to force out the icing. Draw lines and blobs to suggest clothes and facial features.

3 While the icing is still soft, position sugar balls to form eyes, mouths, buttons, and decorative edgings. Let the icing set before threading cord through the hole.

GOLD & SILVER COOKIES
Paint a baked cookie with egg white, then float a sheet of gold or silver leaf onto it.

Countdown to Christmas 78

CHRISTMAS TREE QUARTET

IF YOU HAVE A CLIPPED TREE growing in a pot out in your garden, bring it inside for Christmas. Boxwood, bay, yew, hemlock, privet, and holly all can be grown in containers and adapted as Christmas trees for the holiday season. Or make a mop-headed tree (SEE BELOW) from sprigs of holly and a chicken-wire frame.

Top-knot Tree
WHAT YOU NEED
Clipped boxwood tree
12 in (30 cm) diameter
terracotta pot
6 handfuls silver lichen
30 red fabric roses, in 3 sizes
10 ft (3 m) gathered red ribbon
1 strand white lights

TOP-KNOT TREE
A boxwood tree trained into top-knots makes an extraordinary Christmas tree. Accentuate the tiny, dark green leaves with red roses and twirls of ribbon, and use white lights to add pinpoints of brightness.

Variegated holly

White light

Clipped boxwood tree

Gathered red ribbon

Sheet moss

Silver lichen

Mop-headed Holly
WHAT YOU NEED
20 x 12 in (51 x 30 cm)
  chicken wire
8 in (20 cm) diameter ball wet
  florist's foam, soaked
Spool wire
16 in (41 cm) diameter plastic pot
Plaster of Paris mix
4 ft (1.2 m) branch
18 in (46 cm) diameter decorative pot
3 handfuls sheet moss
120 sprigs holly
1 strand white lights

MOP-HEADED HOLLY
Wrap chicken wire around the foam. Secure with spool wire. Fill the plastic pot with wet plaster of Paris, and set the branch into it. When the plaster is dry, put the pot into the decorative pot. Cover the plaster with moss. Spike the sphere onto the branch and cover with holly. Decorate with lights.

Perfect Pyramid
WHAT YOU NEED
Neat, pyramidal conifer
24 in (61 cm) square
lead container
40 ornaments
15 tissue-paper flowers
(SEE PAGES 22–23)
1 strand colored lights

Owl decoration

Bay tree

Robin decoration

Tissue-paper flower

Neat, pyramidal conifer

Silver ornament

Gold ball

Multi-colored ornament

PERFECT PYRAMID
The dense foliage of this conifer pyramid is adorned with hot-pink, tissue-paper flowers, harlequin and silver spheres, and a strand of colored lights to make a sophisticated Christmas tree.

Bay Tree of Birds
WHAT YOU NEED
Bay tree
20 in (51 cm) square terracotta pot
15 handfuls sphagnum moss
10 multi-colored ornaments
10 gold ornaments
1 strand white lights
7 robin decorations
3 owl decorations

BAY TREE OF BIRDS
The simple beauty of this delicate bay tree is enhanced by its plaited stem. I chose glittering, textured sequins and shiny ornaments to complement the almost matte-like surface of the leaves, while robins and owls add a whimsical touch.

Harlequin ornament

Sphagnum moss

Lead container

Square terracotta pot

Countdown to Christmas 80

COOKIE SELECTION

A SNACK OF CHRISTMAS cookies with tea, coffee, or hot chocolate can be a great family occasion during the festive season. Simple lemon and ginger cookies are perfect, decorated with either icing and sugar balls or bright color glazes, a job that children love. Tempting bite-size wreaths, topped with cherries and gold and silver sugar balls, are show stoppers, so is the sticky nut brittle. More elegant delicacies include brandy snaps that are tipped with bitter chocolate and filled with whipped cream; rich, chocolate Florentines; and tiny tartlets piled with glazed fruits.

LEMON COOKIES
1 stick (115 g) butter
⅓ cup (75 g) superfine sugar
Grated rind of 1 lemon
1½ cups (170 g) all-purpose flour
1 large egg yolk and food coloring
    to glaze

Cream the butter and sugar until fluffy. Stir in the lemon rind and flour. Roll the dough to ⅛ in (3 mm) thickness and cut shapes with cookie cutters. Make holes for hanging the cookies. Place on a buttered baking sheet. Divide the egg yolk between 3 small bowls, and add ½ tsp different food coloring to each. Paint the cookies and bake at 350° F (175°C) for 12 minutes, until lightly browned. Makes 40.

NUT BRITTLE
1 lb (455 g) mixed pistachios, cashews,
    almonds, and hazelnuts
2 cups (455 g) superfine sugar

Toast the nuts and arrange them in a 13 x 9 in (33 x 23 cm) oiled baking pan. Slowly melt the sugar in a heavy saucepan over low heat, stirring constantly until it has melted but not caramelized. Pour the syrup over the nuts; do not stir. When the brittle has cooled, unmold and cut or break into pieces. Makes 18.

Fruit Tartlet

Nut Brittle

Egg glaze

Toasted nuts

Lemon Cookie

FRUIT TARTLETS
¼ cup (55 g) superfine sugar
1 whole large egg plus 1 egg yolk
2 tbs cornstarch
2½ cups (590 ml) milk
½ tsp vanilla extract
1 package pie crust mix
Lightly poached fruit and apricot jam

To make the custard: Whisk the sugar, egg, and egg yolk until light and fluffy. Whisk in the cornstarch, and then the milk and vanilla extract. Bring the mixture just below boiling in a saucepan over low heat. Stir constantly for 2 minutes, until the custard coats the back of a spoon. Cover with a piece of waxed paper and leave to cool.

   Make pastry and roll to ⅛ in (3 mm) thickness. Line buttered tartlet pans with the pastry. Fill with dry beans and bake at 400° F (200° C) for 15 minutes. Remove the beans. When the pastry cools, spoon in custard. Decorate with fruit and glaze the tartlets with warm apricot jam. Makes 30.

FLORENTINES

6 oz (170 g) baking chocolate
5 oz (130 g) mixture of toasted
   almonds, hazelnuts, and pecans;
   glacé cherries; kumquats; orange
   and lemon peel, and crystallized
   violets

Melt the chocolate in a bowl
over a saucepan of simmering
water. Carefully pour chocolate
by tablespoons onto waxed
paper. Arrange the nuts, fruit,
peel, and violets on the
chocolate before it sets. Peel off
the paper when set. Makes 15.

COOKIE WREATHS

6 tbs (85 g) butter
3 cups (170 g) marshmallows
4 drops vanilla extract
1 tsp green food coloring
3 cups (115 g) cornflakes
Glacé cherries and silver and gold
   sugar balls to decorate

Melt the butter in a heavy saucepan
over low heat. Add the marshmallows
and stir until melted. Stir in the vanilla
extract and food coloring, then mix in
the cornflakes. Drop tablespoonfuls
of the mixture onto waxed paper
and press a hole in the middle.
Decorate while still soft. Makes 12.

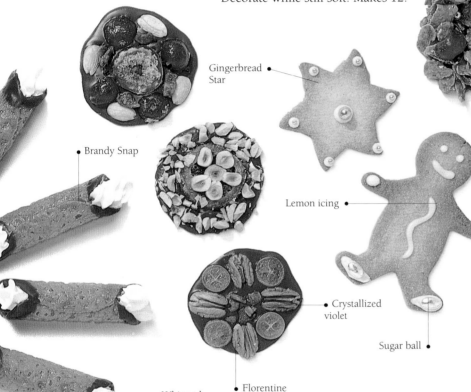

Cookie Wreath

Glacé cherry

Gingerbread Star

Brandy Snap

Lemon icing

Crystallized violet

Sugar ball

Gingerbread Man

Whipped cream

Florentine

BRANDY SNAPS

1½ sticks (170 g) unsalted butter
1 cup (235 ml) corn syrup
¼ cup (55 g) sugar
1 tsp ground ginger
1½ cups (170 g) all-purpose flour
1 tbs brandy
Melted chocolate and whipped cream
   to serve

Place the first 4 ingredients in a
saucepan and bring to a boil, stirring

constantly. Beat in the flour and
brandy. Drop tablespoonfuls onto a
buttered baking sheet, at 4 in (10 cm)
intervals. Bake at 350° F (175° C) for
8 minutes. Allow to cool for 1 minute,
then wrap each cookie around the
oiled handle of a wooden spoon. If the
cookies harden while shaping, return
them to the oven. When cooled, dip
the ends in melted chocolate. Just
before serving, pipe whipped cream
into the centers. Makes 25.

GINGERBREAD COOKIES

1 stick (115 g) butter
½ cup (115 g) brown sugar
¼ cup (90 g) molasses
1 large egg
2½ cups (285 g) all-purpose flour
1 tsp baking powder
2 tsp ground ginger
1 tsp ground cinnamon
Lemon icing and sugar balls to decorate

Cream the butter and sugar. Add the
molasses and egg, and mix until
smooth. Stir in the flour, baking
powder, and spices, and mix to form
a stiff dough. Chill for 1 hour. Roll
out to ⅛ in (3 mm) thickness and cut
shapes with cookie cutters. Place on a
buttered baking sheet. Bake at 350° F
(175° C) for 10 minutes. When cool,
decorate the cookies. Makes 35.

Sugared Flowers & Fruit

CHRISTMAS IS THE SEASON to indulge in exceedingly sweet treats. Sugared flowers and fruits sparkle under a crisp dusting of crystals that shimmer enticingly in the light and tingle on the tongue. A surprising number of flowers and leaves are delicious to eat: roses, primroses, pansies, fruit tree blossoms, mimosa flowers, not to mention the numerous varieties of mint that are particularly good. Whole or sectioned fruit under a veil of sugar also make beautiful decorations, delectable and irresistible.

WHAT YOU NEED
1 egg white
Small paintbrush
½ lb (230 g) edible flowers, leaves, and fruit
½ cup (115 g) granulated sugar

METHOD
Lightly beat the egg white. Using a paintbrush, cover the surfaces of each flower, leaf, or fruit with egg white, taking care not to saturate. Place on waxed paper and sift sugar over to cover evenly. Let dry in a warm place for 2 to 3 hours. Sugared this way, flowers last in perfect condition for several days, and fruit keeps as long as when it is fresh.

• Kumquat

• Lime

• Black fig

Red plum •

• Turkish delight

FLORAL SWEETS
Decorate bought or homemade fruit-and-nut nougat with delicately sugared rose petals and primrose flowers.

Nougat •

PYRAMID OF FRUIT
Large red plums, luscious black figs, limes (to squeeze over the figs), and sharp, bite-sized kumquats make up the glistening pyramid of delicately sugared fruit. Choose only the most perfect-looking fruit for the arrangement.

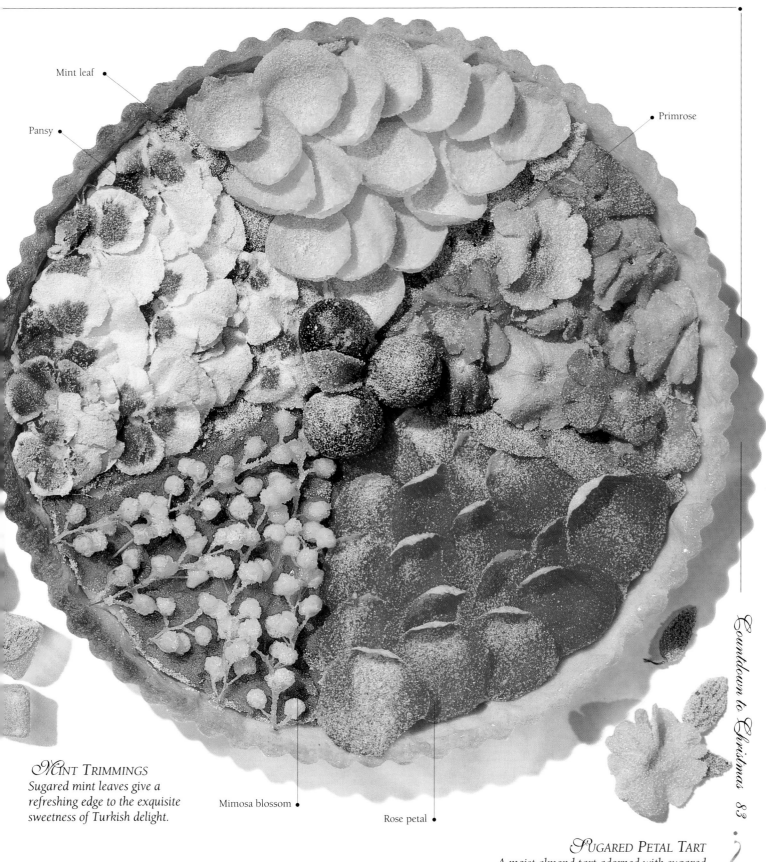

Mint leaf

Pansy

Primrose

MINT TRIMMINGS
*Sugared mint leaves give a
refreshing edge to the exquisite
sweetness of Turkish delight.*

Mimosa blossom

Rose petal

SUGARED PETAL TART
*A moist almond tart adorned with sugared
pansies, mimosa, primroses, and rose petals.
Arranged in the form of a flower, each of its
five "petals" is edged with sugared mint leaves.*

Victorian Molded Desserts

GELATINS ARE GREATLY underrated desserts. I'd like to elevate homemade gelatins to a place near the top of the dessert hierarchy. They can be as refreshing and cool as a sorbet or as rich and creamy as a mousse. Made in a decorative mold, they can also look spectacular. A few practical techniques are essential for a perfect result. Before making the gelatin, oil the mold liberally and place it in the refrigerator for at least one hour. To prepare the gelatin, soften it in cold water, without stirring, for five minutes. When it is spongy, heat carefully until melted, shaking gently without stirring. For large or tall molds, use a little more gelatin for extra stability, but not too much or it will be too stiff.

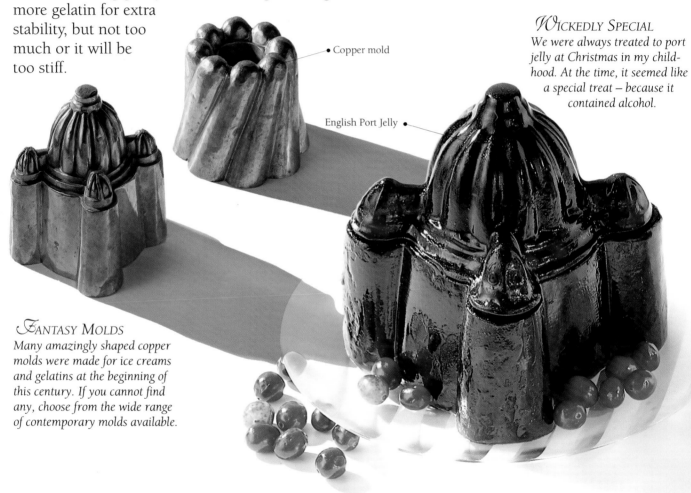

• Copper mold

English Port Jelly •

Wickedly Special
We were always treated to port jelly at Christmas in my child-hood. At the time, it seemed like a special treat – because it contained alcohol.

Fantasy Molds
Many amazingly shaped copper molds were made for ice creams and gelatins at the beginning of this century. If you cannot find any, choose from the wide range of contemporary molds available.

English Port Jelly
¾ oz (20 g) gelatin in 3 tbs water
Grated rind and juice of
  1 large lemon
1½ cups (355 ml) water
½ cinnamon stick
4 cloves
¾ cup (170 g) superfine sugar
1¼ cups (295 ml) port
½ cup (55 g) fresh, or crystallized
  cranberries (SEE PAGES 38–39)

Prepare the gelatin (SEE ABOVE). Place the lemon rind and juice, water, cinnamon, cloves, and sugar in a saucepan and bring to a boil. Remove from the heat and add the melted gelatin. Let cool for 20 minutes, then stir in the port. Strain, and allow to almost set. Pour half of the gelatin into an oiled 4 cup (945 ml) mold and float the cranberries on the surface. Refrigerate until set. Pour the remaining gelatin over the cranberry layer. Refrigerate overnight. Remove 2 hours before serving; unmold an hour before. Serves 6.

FLUMMERY

1 oz (30 g) gelatin in ½ cup
  (120 ml) water
Grated rind and juice of
  1 lemon
4 large eggs
¼ cup (55 g) superfine sugar
2 cups (475 ml) dry sherry
A pinch of nutmeg

Prepare the gelatin (SEE LEFT), then add cold water to make up to 2 cups (475 ml). Stir in the lemon rind and juice. Mix the eggs, sugar, sherry, and nutmeg, and add to the melted gelatin. Heat in a double boiler until it coats the back of a spoon. Strain into an oiled 4 cup (945 ml) mold and refrigerate over-night. Remove 2 hours before serving; unmold an hour before. Serves 8.

Flummery •

ANCIENT TASTE
Flummery, a very old recipe made with rich sherry custard flavored with lemon, has a traditional Christmas taste.

MOCHA CREAM

Chocolate Gelatin:
4 large egg yolks
½ cup (115 g) superfine sugar
¼ cup cocoa powder
2 cups (475 ml) milk
2 tbs rum
½ oz (15 g) gelatin in 2 tbs
  water
⅔ cup (160 ml) whipping
  cream, whipped

Coffee Gelatin:
2 cups (475 ml) coffee
½ cup (115 g) superfine sugar
½ oz (15 g) gelatin in 2 tbs
  water
2 tbs coffee liqueur
Rum-flavored cream to serve

Make the chocolate gelatin. Beat the egg yolks, sugar, and cocoa powder until creamy. Heat the milk to just below boiling, then whisk into the egg-yolk mixture. Heat in a double-boiler until it coats the back of a spoon. Remove from the heat and stir in the rum. When cool, stir in the melted gelatin (SEE LEFT). Allow to almost set, then fold in the whipped cream.

Make the coffee gelatin. Heat the coffee and sugar. Stir in the melted gelatin and coffee liqueur and leave until almost set. Pour half of the chocolate gelatin into an oiled 4 cup (945 ml) mold. Let set, then pour in half of the coffee gelatin. Repeat to make 2 more layers. Refrigerate overnight. Remove 2 hours before serving; unmold an hour before. Pass rum-flavored cream separately. Serves 6.

Mocha Cream •

MOCHA FLAVOR
Dark chocolate and coffee layers form a cool and creamy mocha gelatin with a simply delicious flavor.

CHOCOLATE TRUFFLES

TRUFFLES OF THE CHOCOLATE KIND have to be one of the most delicious and wicked treats of all time. They seem more "chocolatey" than chocolate and "creamier" than cream. With the added flavors of brandy, rum, or another favorite liqueur, they are an indulgence that is absolutely essential at Christmas time. Commercial truffles are good, but these homemade ones are unforgettable. They can all be made a month in advance and frozen.

• Pink Champagne Truffles

VANILLA TRUFFLES
To make these truffles, follow the recipe for Cream Truffles, but add ½ tsp of vanilla extract instead of liqueur. You can then coat the truffles with melted white chocolate.

• Rum Truffles dusted with confectioners' sugar

BUTTERY TRUFFLES
10 oz (285 g) baking chocolate
1 stick (115 g) unsalted butter
¼ cup (60 ml) water
1 large egg yolk, lightly beaten
1 tbs flavoring (brandy, rum, other
  liqueurs, or espresso coffee)
Cocoa powder, confectioners' sugar,
  or instant coffee powder to decorate

Break the chocolate into small pieces and heat with the butter and water in a double boiler, stirring until smooth. Stir in the egg yolk and flavoring. Pour into a 6 in (15 cm) square pan lined with waxed paper. Refrigerate until set. Remove from the pan by the paper, and cut into squares or mold into balls. Roll or dust the truffles in cocoa powder, confectioners' sugar, or a mixture of confectioners' sugar and coffee powder. Refrigerate for a week or freeze for up to a month. Makes 35.

DOUBLE-DIPPED TRUFFLES
Cream Truffles flavored with Grand Marnier are double-dipped in dark and white chocolate. Prepare two bowls of melted chocolate, one dark and one white. Skewer each truffle. Dip half in the white chocolate, let set, and then dip the other half in dark chocolate.

CREAM TRUFFLES
10 oz (285 g) baking chocolate
1 stick (115 g) unsalted butter
1¼ cups (295 ml) heavy cream
2 tbs flavoring (brandy, rum, other
liqueurs, or espresso coffee)

Break the chocolate into small pieces and melt with the butter in a double boiler, stirring until smooth. Warm the cream to just below boiling, and stir into the chocolate mixture. Add the flavoring and let cool. Freeze until solid. Remove from the freezer and scoop into balls, about ¾ in (2 cm) in diameter. Dip the truffles in melted chocolate (SEE ABOVE RIGHT) and let cool. Truffles will keep for a week in the refrigerator, or up to a month in the freezer. Makes 20.

RUM TRUFFLES
Buttery Truffles can be
flavored with dark rum,
and rolled in cocoa powder.

PINK CHAMPAGNE TRUFFLES
Cream Truffles flavored with Champagne
liqueur are coated in melted white chocolate,
lightly tinted with pink food coloring.

COATING CREAM TRUFFLES
Prepare a bowl of melted dark or white
chocolate. Skewer a Cream Truffle and dip
it in the chocolate to coat completely. Lift
it out, twirling the tail of chocolate to the
side of the truffle. Slip the skewer through
the wires of a rack until the truffle rests
on it, then pull to remove the skewer.
Repeat for the rest
of the truffles.

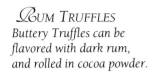

TIA MARIA TRUFFLES
The delicious coffee flavor
of Tia Maria in the Buttery
Truffles is echoed by a
dusting of instant
coffee powder
mixed with
confectioners' sugar.

• Cream Truffles
dipped in dark
chocolate

NUTTY TRUFFLES
Dip amaretto-flavored
Cream Truffles in melted
chocolate mixed with
chopped, toasted
almonds.

CHOCOLATE WATERLILY
Melt 12 oz (340 g) white or
dark chocolate and 3 tbs
maple syrup in a double
boiler. When cool, press
into petal shapes. Pour
1 tsp melted chocolate
into a teacup lined with
plastic wrap. Slightly furl
each chocolate petal and
arrange in the cup: layer

the petals from the
outside inward. Finish
with two twirled petals
in the center. Remove
the completed chocolate
waterlily when set.

PETITS FOURS

PETITS FOURS, LITTLE SWEETS eaten with coffee at the end of a meal, are perilous delights that lie somewhere between cakes and confectionery. The French king, Louis XVI, who is known to have enjoyed them, gave them their name ("little oven" in English). The original petits fours were small sponge cakes, but now they give their name to any little sweet delicacies.

I have always liked fruit-based petits fours because they clear the palate after a rich meal. Little fluted cookies filled with raspberries and various fruit dipped in fondants and dark and white chocolates are a perfect finale to a special dinner.

RASPBERRIES IN TULIPS
Whisk 3 egg whites until just mixed. Stir in 1¼ cups (200 g) flour and 1 cup (115 g) confectioners' sugar, then 1 stick (115 g) cooled, melted butter. Place teaspoonfuls of the batter onto a buttered baking sheet and spread very thinly to form 3 in (7.5 cm) circles. Bake at 425° F (220° C) for 3 minutes, until golden. Mold each biscuit over an upturned egg cup to form a fluted cookie. Before serving, fill with raspberries dusted with confectioners' sugar. Makes 40.

STUFFED PRUNES
Stuff Armagnac- or brandy-soaked prunes with apricot purée (SEE PAGE 37) or marzipan – make roses from thin strips rolled into coils.

• Marzipan-stuffed prune

Fondant-dipped • Cape gooseberry

Fondant-dipped • strawberry

Fondant-dipped • kumquat

FONDANT-DIPPED FRUIT
Gently heat 8 oz (225 g) ready-made fondant in a double-boiler, stirring with a wooden spoon. Add 1 tbs kirsch or brandy, if you wish. If necessary, stir in some corn syrup to thin. Holding fruit such as strawberries and kumquats by the stem, dip each piece into the fondant and place right side up on waxed paper to set. Covers about 40.

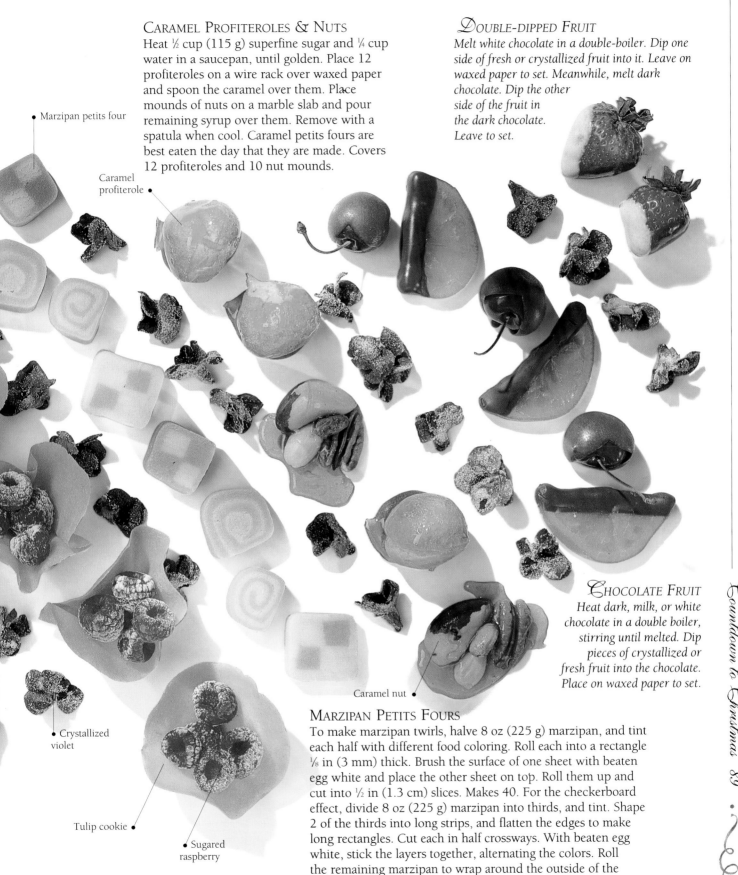

CARAMEL PROFITEROLES & NUTS

Heat ½ cup (115 g) superfine sugar and ¼ cup water in a saucepan, until golden. Place 12 profiteroles on a wire rack over waxed paper and spoon the caramel over them. Place mounds of nuts on a marble slab and pour remaining syrup over them. Remove with a spatula when cool. Caramel petits fours are best eaten the day that they are made. Covers 12 profiteroles and 10 nut mounds.

DOUBLE-DIPPED FRUIT

Melt white chocolate in a double-boiler. Dip one side of fresh or crystallized fruit into it. Leave on waxed paper to set. Meanwhile, melt dark chocolate. Dip the other side of the fruit in the dark chocolate. Leave to set.

• Marzipan petits four

Caramel
profiterole •

CHOCOLATE FRUIT

Heat dark, milk, or white chocolate in a double boiler, stirring until melted. Dip pieces of crystallized or fresh fruit into the chocolate. Place on waxed paper to set.

Caramel nut •

• Crystallized
violet

Tulip cookie •

• Sugared
raspberry

MARZIPAN PETITS FOURS

To make marzipan twirls, halve 8 oz (225 g) marzipan, and tint each half with different food coloring. Roll each into a rectangle ⅛ in (3 mm) thick. Brush the surface of one sheet with beaten egg white and place the other sheet on top. Roll them up and cut into ½ in (1.3 cm) slices. Makes 40. For the checkerboard effect, divide 8 oz (225 g) marzipan into thirds, and tint. Shape 2 of the thirds into long strips, and flatten the edges to make long rectangles. Cut each in half crossways. With beaten egg white, stick the layers together, alternating the colors. Roll the remaining marzipan to wrap around the outside of the checkered marzipan. Cut into ½ in (1.3 cm) slices. Makes 40.

Chapter Three

LAST-MINUTE CREATIONS

THE GREAT DAY has arrived. A list of
everything that needs to be done helps
enormously – it is the only way that I remember
to arrange flowers waiting in a bucket, chill the
white wine, and serve the cheese or a salad I
have already made. It is certainly easier to
have the feast in the evening, so that there
is ample time for preparation. Remember,
the main aim is to enjoy the day, so have
plenty of happy helpers on hand.

FRESH AND FRAGRANT
Perfumed deep red and white roses, white tulips,
spicy-scented lilies, sprays of pale pink and gold
orchids, fatsia leaves, and the intriguing kangaroo
paw flowers spill out of a flared and fluted vase
in festive disarray. A starry background
dramatically offsets the arrangement.

Tartan Stockings

WHEN I WAS A CHILD, waiting for my stocking on Christmas Eve was almost unbearable. I slept fitfully and, consequently, was tired and rather bad-tempered on Christmas day. My favorite stocking was big enough to take a hefty present as well as plenty of stocking fillers. At least one unwrapped present was always at the top, giving an exciting hint of the treats to come!

Corals and Blue
A stocking in shades of coral pink and cornflower blue, with matching trim, bulges with hidden "goodies." A knitted Piglet, ears flying, waits eagerly to be picked up, while the tangerine will sustain you as you explore the stocking's contents.

Candy cane

Seasonal Stripes
A teddy bear and tiny present peep from the top of this red and green striped stocking, tempting the recipient to look further. The stocking's stripes are quilted, with a cuff of horizontal stripes. A jolly red-and-green bow and cord piping add a final flourish.

Rich Reds & Golds
This red and gold tartan stocking, quilted diagonally, has a cuff of bright red satin edged with satin cord. Inside, a toy soldier and twirled candy canes wait for some lucky child.

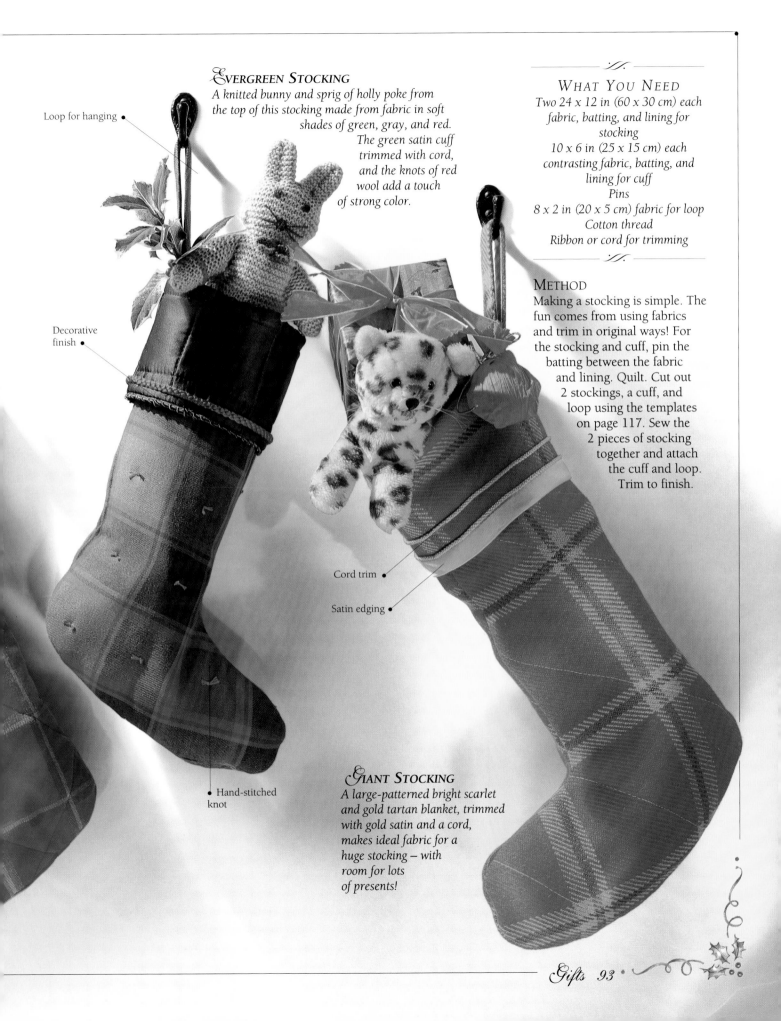

Evergreen Stocking

A knitted bunny and sprig of holly poke from the top of this stocking made from fabric in soft shades of green, gray, and red. The green satin cuff trimmed with cord, and the knots of red wool add a touch of strong color.

Loop for hanging

Decorative finish

Hand-stitched knot

Cord trim

Satin edging

— *⁄⁄.* —

What You Need

Two 24 x 12 in (60 x 30 cm) each fabric, batting, and lining for stocking
10 x 6 in (25 x 15 cm) each contrasting fabric, batting, and lining for cuff
Pins
8 x 2 in (20 x 5 cm) fabric for loop
Cotton thread
Ribbon or cord for trimming

— *⁄⁄.* —

Method

Making a stocking is simple. The fun comes from using fabrics and trim in original ways! For the stocking and cuff, pin the batting between the fabric and lining. Quilt. Cut out 2 stockings, a cuff, and loop using the templates on page 117. Sew the 2 pieces of stocking together and attach the cuff and loop. Trim to finish.

Giant Stocking

A large-patterned bright scarlet and gold tartan blanket, trimmed with gold satin and a cord, makes ideal fabric for a huge stocking – with room for lots of presents!

DECORATIVE GIFT BOXES

WHEN CHOOSING GIFT BOXES, I recommend that you buy the more complicated ones, then add decorations of your own. Simpler boxes, however, are easy to prepare if you use the templates given (SEE PAGE 117). Paste your own choice of wrapping paper, or even decorative pages from a magazine, to the card stock used to make the boxes. Alternatively, make small bags from pretty fabrics in any colors or patterns you like.

TALL TRIANGLES
I always enjoy looking through old magazines for photographs and illustrations to cover boxes. I cut out red paper berries with a hole puncher and glued them to the black and white design.

TIDY BUNDLE
A jewel-like, glazed fabric tied with a brilliant green bow makes ideal wrapping for a small present. If the gift is light enough, hang it from the boughs of the Christmas tree.

• Corn yellow paper ribbon

• Hot-pink dried peony

MIRO CASKET
A reproduction of a Miró painting covers this attractive casket-shaped gift box.

• Tile-look picture from a magazine

PATTERNED PYRAMIDS
Fill small, patterned pyramid boxes with candy, truffles, or Turkish delight to hang from the Christmas tree. If you need a hanging loop, thread a darning needle with ribbon or cord and pierce it through the top of the box. Tie the ribbon ends.

RIOTOUS COLORS

Liberally decorate and seal your boxed presents with bows (SEE PAGES 96–97). Ready-made square and rectangular boxes wrapped in gift papers demand matching or clashing ribbons, tapes, and strings. Let your imagination run wild with colors and textures because, at Christmas, anything goes.

Gilt red ribbon

Gold-covered cord

Royal blue taffeta with a green sheen

FLOWER DECORATION

A dried peony makes a flouncy centerpiece for the lid of this oval box. Unrumple the petals of dried flowers by gently steaming them open. Use only a little steam from the spout of a kettle or the flower will collapse.

CHRISTMAS WRAPS

FOLLOW THESE GIFT-WRAPPING techniques to give your carefully chosen presents the perfect finishing touch before placing them under the tree.

✂. FABRIC WRAPPING .✂

1 Cut a square large enough to rest the present on from a piece of cardboard. Cut out a circle with a diameter about 5 times the width of the cardboard square from a stiff piece of fabric.

2 Place the present on the cardboard, then center it on the fabric. Gather up the fabric in pleats, and tie firmly with a piece of ribbon to close the package. Attach a bow for a final flourish.

✂. PAPER WRAPPING .✂

1 Use paper long enough to wrap around the box with a few inches overlap. The paper's width should be 1½ times the width of the box. Secure one end of the paper to the top of the box with double-sided tape. Make a fold along the other end for a neat seam.

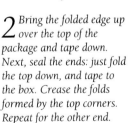

2 Bring the folded edge up over the top of the package and tape down. Next, seal the ends: just fold the top down, and tape to the box. Crease the folds formed by the top corners. Repeat for the other end.

3 Fold both creased corners in against the box and tape down. Then fold up the final flap and tape. Repeat on the other end.

ℱANCY ℬOWS

USE RIBBONS IN A MEDLEY of exciting materials and all the colors of the rainbow to make the most sumptuous bows. Tied and twisted into a myriad of brilliantly colored loops and banners, bows add that final touch to Christmas trees, garlands, wreaths, and Christmas presents.

Prepare bows for the Christmas tree or for garlands well in advance, but it is best to tie your bows for presents after they have been wrapped, so that you can be sure that each bow matches its box.

Double bow • of wire-edged silver and blue ribbons

• Single bow of gold-edged red ribbon

ℐINGLE ℬOWS
Use one length of ribbon to make a single bow with two pairs of overlapping loops, both twisted into figure-eights, and two trailing ends, neatened with diagonal cuts.

• Single bow of mauve metallic ribbon

Double bow of • paper and striped grosgrain ribbons

RIBBON-TYING METHODS

USE THE BASIC METHOD for single, double, and rosette bows. Keep loops open and centers tightly gathered.

✄ BASIC METHOD ✄

1 *Unroll some of the ribbon and loop one end over the remainder. Hold in place with your thumb and forefinger.*

2 *With more ribbon, form the second loop of the bow, and bring the rest of the ribbon back over the top to make an X-shape at the center.*

3 *Now make a third loop, using more of the ribbon, and bringing the long end over the front of the bow.*

4 *Make another loop and bring the end back over the middle of the bow to make the second X-shape.*

DOUBLE BOWS

Make a double bow with two or more ribbons, using the technique for a single bow. It is ideal for large presents.

MULTI-LOOP BOWS

Bows made with thin ribbon, string, or cord look best if they have masses of loops and twirling ends.

• Rosette bow of star-printed royal blue silk ribbon

Rosette bow of pink- and wire-edged green silk ribbon •

• Multi-loop bow in loops of thin pastel ribbon

• Rosette bow of striped silk ribbon

Multi-loop bow of • metallic ribbons

Rosette bow of wire-edged pink-and-orange rainbow taffeta

ROSETTE BOWS

Create a rosette-like bow by continuing either the single or double ribbon-tying method to form several more loops. The finished ribbon has loops falling in all directions and resembles a flower.

---

5 Pleat the center of the bow with your fingers, working from the center outward in both directions.

6 Secure the bow's center with a length of spool wire or narrow ribbon. Open the loops and arrange the trailing ends.

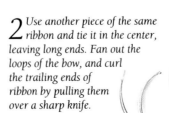

⚜ MULTI-LOOP BOW ⚜

1 Make several loops around your hand with a long piece of thin ribbon, string, or cord. Keep holding it while you remove your hand, then twist it in the center to form a figure-eight.

2 Use another piece of the same ribbon and tie it in the center, leaving long ends. Fan out the loops of the bow, and curl the trailing ends of ribbon by pulling them over a sharp knife.

TREE OF FLOWERS

IN A SENSE, a decorated Christmas tree is like a large flower arrangement. This thought inspired me to try covering a tree with flowers. The idea sounded glorious but flowers out of water have a short life. So, I arranged them in cellophane bags, pots, and baskets with water or wet foam. This way, the flowers last for a week or more.

FRESH FLOWER POSIES
Cornflowers, gypsophila, and a tulip, wrapped in a water-filled cellophane cone and tied with a blue ribbon.

TERRACOTTA POTS
Glue cord to the rim of a flower-filled terracotta pot. Make a simple harness for the larger pots.

FLOWER BASKETS
Attach generous loops to the basket handles so that the flowers do not become entangled in the branches.

WHAT YOU NEED
For a 6 ft (1.8 m) tree:
17 in (43 cm) diameter
  fluted terracotta pot
2 strands white lights
3 bunches gypsophila
60 cornflowers
40 tulips
30 delphiniums
30 grape hyacinths
30 proteas
8 yd (7 m) smilax vine
40 anemones
20 tiny terracotta pots
15 small terracotta pots
30 small baskets
1 plastic garbage bag
Six 9 x 4½ x 3 in (23 x 11 x
  8 cm) bricks wet florist's foam
Twenty 12 x 9 in (30 x
  23 cm) cellophane squares
3 ft (1 m) ribbon
3 ft (1 m) gold cord

MINIATURE ARRANGEMENTS

CHOOSE LIGHT CONTAINERS to hold your fresh flower arrangements. Once the baskets, pots, and cellophane are filled with water, they weigh considerably more.

✂. FLOWER-FILLED BASKETS & POTS ✂.

1 Measure and cut circles of plastic to line the inside of each container. The diameter of each circle should be twice the height plus the width of the base of the container. Wedge small cubes of soaked, wet foam in the containers to hold the lining.

2 Tie a loop of ribbon to the handle of each basket, and glue a loop of cord to the rim of each pot.

3 Push the stems of the flowers into the foam. Keep the arrangement low to prevent it from becoming top-heavy.

✂. CELLOPHANE-WRAPPED FLOWERS ✂.

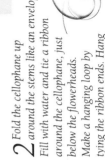

1 Make a small bunch of flowers with stems 4 in (10 cm) long, removing all leaves from the lower halves of the stems. Place the flowers on a corner of a 12 x 9 in (30 x 23 cm) piece of clear cellophane.

2 Fold the cellophane up around the stems like an envelope. Fill with water and tie a ribbon around the cellophane, just below the flowerheads. Make a hanging loop by tying the ribbon ends. Hang to test for watertightness.

Smilax Vine
Smilax vine is a delicate climber. Trim and place in water before making garlands.

Frosty Gypsophila
I have used gypsophila in all the arrangements on this Christmas tree. Its delicate, frosty white flowers have a honeylike scent.

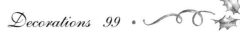

ROSEMARY & MIMOSA DESIGN

FOR PEOPLE WHO CELEBRATE CHRISTMAS in the cold and dark days of winter, it's pleasing to think that spring is not so far away. In the weeks before Christmas, stores are full of spring flowers: tulips, daffodils, hyacinths, and mimosa, as well as all the year-round favorites such as roses, lilies, and freesias. Of course, for those in the warmer climates, the choice of flowers and foliage is always overwhelming at Christmas.

Take advantage of either the early spring or luscious summer flowers to create a sunny yellow arrangement for the holiday – it makes a welcome change from the traditional reds and greens. Here, I have arranged sweetly perfumed flowers in the shape of a miniature tree and a complementary swag. Although roses, ranunculus, dill, yellow peppers, and rosemary may seem an odd mix, their perfumes and shapes mingle deliciously, and they look as if they were always meant for each other.

Mimosa •

Dill •

Rose •

Swag
WHAT YOU NEED
4 ft x 6 in (120 x 15 cm) chicken wire
12 handfuls damp moss
70 sprigs mimosa
40 sprigs rosemary
24 yellow roses
20 stems flowering dill
15 clusters yellow peppers
Two 12 x 6 in (30 x 15 cm) chicken wire
Spool wire

METHOD
Make a moss-filled roll with the longer piece of chicken wire and 8 handfuls of the damp moss (SEE PAGE 57, STEPS 1 AND 2). Shape the roll into 2 curves for the horizontal part of the swag. Using two-thirds of the plant material, stick the stems into the wire frame, starting from the ends and working to the middle. Make 2 smaller moss-filled rolls with the remaining chicken wire and moss, to form the vertical lengths of the swag. Insert the remaining flowers and foliage, working from the bottom to the top. Finish by securing the vertical pieces to the horizontal part of the swag with spool wire.

Miniature Tree
WHAT YOU NEED
6 in (15 cm) diameter plastic pot
7 in (18 cm) square terracotta pot
Plaster of Paris mix
16 in (40 cm) long birch branch
5 x 3½ x 3 in (13 x 9 x 7.5 cm) brick wet florist's foam, soaked
16 in (40 cm) square chicken wire
Spool wire
45 sprigs mimosa
18 yellow roses
18 white ranunculus
12 stems flowering dill
5 handfuls live green moss

METHOD
Place the plastic pot inside the terracotta pot. Pour wet plaster of Paris into the plastic pot. Push the branch into the wet plaster and prop it into position until the plaster sets. Carve a hole in the foam brick so that it can sit on top of the branch. Cover the foam with chicken wire, securing it with spool wire. Arrange the flowers in the foam and cover the plaster of Paris with live moss.

LONG-LASTING SWAG
This sweet-smelling golden swag would look lovely on a
wall above a side table or mantelpiece. Make it as long
or as tall as you wish. The swag will keep for months
because, once you remove the roses, the other
flowers and foliage slowly dry out, developing
a softer, faded look.

• Yellow
pepper

• Unripe,
yellow
pepper

Birch •
branch

Live moss •

Ranunculus •

• Rosemary

FLOWER TREE
The off-centered trunk of this
miniature tree makes it look more
interesting than if it were absolutely
symmetrical. Keep the flowers fresh
by putting a few ice cubes on top of
the foam sphere each day.

Table Centerpiece

FLOWERS FROM ALL OVER THE WORLD are available at Christmas. This is the time to have the most wonderful combination of varieties in a glorious riot of color. I always try to use at least a touch of red in any festive arrangement. This centerpiece has every shade of that splendid color, embracing bright and pale pinks as well as oranges and ambers. Fruit, such as a few grapes or trails of dates, gives any creation an added dimension. Another touch I like is to have a few petals or flowers scattered on the table beside the arrangement; if a flower falls, leave the petals where they lie. Tailor the size and shape of the arrangement to your table, so that the flowers do not get in the way of the food or the guests.

Tulip

Carnation

Amaryllis

Eucalyptus

Euphorbia marginata

WHAT YOU NEED
Floral prong
Glass goblet or vase
Adhesive clay
5 x 3½ x 3 in (13 x 9 x 7.5 cm)
brick wet florist's foam, soaked
Gold or silver spray paint,
or silver moss
Straight floral wires
3 bunches grapes
20 poppies
15 carnations
10 sprigs eucalyptus foliage
10 tulips
8 nerines
7 snapdragons
6 Euphorbia marginata
5 stems 'La Reve' lilies
5 amaryllis
4 orchids

METHOD
Secure the prong in the goblet or vase with adhesive clay. Press the foam onto the prong (spray the sides of the vase gold or silver or line with silver moss to hide the foam.) Wire the grape bunches in first, then add the flowers one by one, so they look as if they are springing from the base of the bowl and cascading over the sides. For a peony-like effect, tie several carnations together just below their flower-heads and use them as one gigantic bloom.

BOUNTEOUS DISPLAY

Bluish pinks, golden oranges, and glorious reds vie with each other to dazzle. The overall effect is a fresh and subtle mélange of colors and shapes. The spicy fragrance of the ice-pink lilies is an added bonus.

• Orchid

• Nerine

• Snapdragon

• Poppy

'La Reve' lily •

• Bunch of grapes

Last-minute Creations 104

Place Settings

A COMBINATION OF BEAUTIFUL FLOWERS and scented candles creates the perfect atmosphere for a memorable dinner party. Individual arrangements of flowers echo the table centerpiece, and some hold candles in their centers. Order your flowers well ahead, because most of the flower shops have sold their most beautiful specimens by Christmas Eve. Organize your time so that you can arrange the flowers at leisure the day before your party.

INDIVIDUAL NOSEGAYS
Small frosted glasses beside each place setting hold little nosegays made up of a few flowers and bits of foliage from the main arrangement.

'Paperwhite' narcissus

Agapanthus

Freesia

Anemone

Napkin Ring
WHAT YOU NEED
3 ft (1 m) wire-edged
silver ribbon
Napkin
Silver thread
2 sprigs ivy
Glue
1 anemone flowerhead

METHOD
Cut the silver ribbon into a 10 in (25 cm) long piece and a 26 in (65 cm) long piece. Knot a loop in the shorter piece to hold the napkin, leaving long ends. From the longer ribbon, make a single bow (SEE PAGES 96–97) with 3 loops, and attach to the other ribbon with silver thread. Trim all the ribbon ends at a slant. About an hour before the meal, tie the ivy together with thread, leaving the ends long. Glue the anemone to the ivy spray and attach to the silver bow with the thread.

Ranunculus •

White
lilac •

MEDLEY OF FLOWERS
*A number of flowers in shades of white,
yellow, pink, red, and lavender are
arranged by color, with stems of ivy
laced through them. Make sure that
some of the flowers are sweetly,
but not overpoweringly, scented.
If you make the centerpiece a
day in advance with very
fresh flowers, it should
last for six days
in a cool place.*

• 'Aladdin' tulip

• Arum lily

FLOWER-RINGED CANDLES
*Each subtly scented bayberry
candle stands in a small, frosted
glass. Water fills the space
between the candle and
glass, to prolong the life
of the ruff of flowers.*

'Mini Heron' ivy •

Carnation •

• Miniature rose

TABLE TRIMMINGS

WHEN PREPARING FOR A SPECIAL Christmas dinner party, bear in mind that it is the extra trimmings that make a table look so marvelously welcoming. In addition to a beautiful flower centerpiece, delicate garlands of ever-greens and berries encircling each plate are entrancing. You can also tie a nosegay of flowers to the back of each chair with a bow. This makes a delightful gift for each guest to take home at the end of the meal.

Prepare the floral centerpiece and chairback nosegays one day ahead, but attach them to the chairs only an hour before the party begins. Plate garlands can be time-consuming to prepare, so make them several hours in advance, and then store in a cool place. If you omit delicate-leaved foliage from the garlands, you can prepare them the day before.

GARLAND AROUND A PLATE
Use plant material and ribbon in traditional Christmas colors to make a small garland for each place setting.

• Variegated ivy

• Douglas fir

• Paper-ribbon bow

Plate Garland
WHAT YOU NEED
Two 12 in (30 cm) straight floral wires
Green floral tape
20 sprigs Douglas fir
15 sprigs variegated miniature-leaved ivy
10 berried sprigs cotoneaster or holly
Spool wire
Red paper-ribbon bow
(SEE PAGES 96–97)
Matching ribbon

METHOD
Twist the ends of the straight floral wires together to form a 24 in (60 cm) length. Cover with the green floral tape. Starting from the left, attach plant material to the floral wire, using spool wire to secure. Allow the plant material to overlap, and cover the ends of each bunch with green floral tape. The greenery and berries look best if you use sprigs of varying lengths. Finish the garland with a festive bow attached with a narrower piece of the same ribbon. Curl the wreath around the plate, leaving space at the front so that it does not prevent your guest from eating!

Spray of miniature green orchids

Anemone

Rose

Douglas fir

FOCAL POINT
A modern, fluted vase makes a perfect container for an informal table centerpiece of green orchids, red anemones, perfumed roses, and Douglas fir. Remember to keep the arrangement low, so that guests can see across the table and talk to each other with ease.

Chairback Nosegay
WHAT YOU NEED

3 red roses
2 red anemones
2 sprays miniature green orchids
1 sprig ivy
4 sprigs Douglas fir
Spool wire
Red paper-ribbon bow
(SEE PAGES 96–97)
Matching ribbon
Safety pins

METHOD
For each place setting, make a small, flat-backed bouquet, binding the stems together with spool wire. Place in water. An hour before the party, remove the bouquets from water and dry the stems. Tie the bow to the front of the nosegay with thin strips of the same ribbon. Leave 2 long ends to secure to the back of the chair. If the chair is upholstered, cut the ribbon ends shorter, and attach the nosegay with 2 small safety pins.

PARTY PUNCHES

PUNCHES ARE AS MUCH A PART OF CHRISTMAS as the tree and the cake. With a little attention to the decoration, they can look extra special. Anyone driving will appreciate light and refreshing non-alcoholic punches, such as the fruit cup flavored with rosehips, citrus fruits, and grape juice. If you prefer some fizz, try the bubbly Champagne cup. I've also included some wickedly strong and rich drinks: an eggnog that's so thick it needs a spoon; a mulled claret that, to me, epitomizes Christmas; and a sophisticated peach-wine and Curaçao concoction.

EGGNOG
6 large eggs, separated
⅓ cup (75 g) superfine sugar
¼ tsp ground nutmeg
⅔ cup (160 ml) brandy or bourbon
1 cup (235 ml) heavy cream
Ground nutmeg to decorate

Beat the egg yolks, sugar, and nutmeg. Add the alcohol and cream. Beat egg whites until stiff, and fold into the eggnog. Chill. Sprinkle with nutmeg. Serves 8.

Star fruit slice

Sugared white grape

Champagne Cup

Sugared glass rim

Eggnog

Mulled Claret

Kiwi fruit slice

Peach Punch

MULLED CLARET

2 cups (475 ml) water
5 cloves
4 allspice
½ cinnamon stick
Rind of 1 orange
2 tsp sugar
1 bottle claret
Twists of orange peel to
  decorate

Bring the water, spices, and
rind to a boil in a large
saucepan over low heat.
Remove from the heat and
add the sugar. Leave for 30
minutes. Strain, then add
the wine. Heat to just below
boiling, then decorate with
orange peel. Serves 8.

PEACH PUNCH

2 bottles peach wine
⅓ cup (80 ml) kirsch
⅓ cup (80 ml) blue
  Curaçao
Juice of ½ lemon
2 white peaches, peeled and
  sliced, to decorate

Mix all the ingredients
together in a punch bowl,
and serve with slices of
peach floating on the
surface. Serves 15.

CHAMPAGNE CUP

2 bottles Champagne
3 cups (710 ml) club soda
1 cup (235 ml) Champagne
  brandy
1 tbs sugar
Sliced star fruit and kiwi fruit,
  and sugared white grapes
  (SEE PAGES 82–83) *to decorate*

Thoroughly chill both the
Champagne and club soda.
Stir all the ingredients
together in a large punch
bowl. Decorate with the
sliced fruit and sugared
grapes. Serve immediately to
make the most of the bubbles!
Serves 15.

FRUIT CUP

⅔ cup (140 g) sugar
3¾ cups (885 ml) each water,
  grape juice, and ginger ale
2 cups (475 ml) each
  red currant juice, strong
  hibiscus tea, and strong
  rosehip tea
Juice of 6 limes, 4 grapefruits,
  and 4 oranges
Crushed ice and fruit to
  decorate

Dissolve the sugar in the
water in a medium sauce-
pan over low heat. When
cooled, pour the syrup into
a large punch bowl and add
the other ingredients. Chill.
When ready to serve, add
the crushed ice and decorate
with fruit such as lychees,
red currants, slices of lime,
kumquat, or pomegranate.
Serves 30.

Sliced lime

Pomegranate slice

Cluster of red currants

Fruit Cup

Sushi Buffet

THE JAPANESE HAVE A HIGH REGARD for both the taste and appearance of food. Sushi, one of the most famous dishes of Japan, tantalizingly delicious and extremely decorative, has become popular around the world. For a festive gathering of family and friends, a buffet of sushi makes a very special and highly original feast. The delicate flavors provide just the change that the palate needs during the Christmas season when richness prevails. Do not be daunted by memories of sushi chefs working at the speed of light. You will be able to produce the decorative dishes set out on these fans with ease. Most of the ingredients are readily available, although you may have to search for dried seaweed sheets. Substitute smoked salmon or trout for the seaweed, if you prefer.

Sushi Rice

½ cup (100 g) short-grain
 white rice
1 cup (235 ml) water
3–4 tbs confectioners' sugar
4–6 tbs distilled malt vinegar
2 tbs ginger, finely chopped
2 tbs garlic, finely chopped

Place the rice and water in a covered saucepan and bring to the boil. Lower the heat to a simmer, and cook for 10–15 minutes, until the rice absorbs all the water, and is sticky. While the rice is hot, stir in the confectioners' sugar, vinegar, ginger, and garlic. It is now ready for shaping into sushi.

Shell of soy sauce

Parsley

Salmon roe

Grated daikon
(white radish)

Sushi Boats

Squeeze sushi rice into small ovals. Mist 8 x 1½ in (20 x 4 cm) strips of dried seaweed sheets, and fold in half, crossways. Shape around the rice, pinching the ends together (the damp seaweed will stick together). Fill with salmon roe or caviar.

Smoked Salmon Parcels

Place small squares of smoked salmon on individual pieces of plastic wrap. Roll sushi rice into little balls and place on top of the salmon. Twist the plastic wrap around the salmon and rice to form tight balls. Chill. When firm, unwrap the balls and garnish with wasabi, ginger, lemon zest, grated daikon, or edible leaves.

Red pepper julienne •

Fresh Greens in Salmon
Humble green beans and spring onions, wrapped in smoked salmon, look and taste quite delicious (SEE BELOW).

Vegetarian Sushi
Baby corn-on-the-cob, green beans, and red peppers nestle in sushi rice, and are wrapped up in a sheet of sea-weed (SEE BELOW). A garnish of edible leaves and lemon zest add to the color.

Lemon zest •

Wasabi paste •

• Ginger paste

Salmon & Seaweed Slices
A sheet of seaweed and marinated salmon encircles sushi rice, green beans, and baby carrots (SEE RIGHT). Serve with condiments, such as horseradish and mustard, and soy sauce in a shell.

Method for Rolling Sushi
This simple technique is quick to learn. Fill the rolls with crunchy and colorful ingredients. Place an 8 x 7 in (20 x 18 cm) dried seaweed sheet on plastic wrap, shiny side down. Mist with water to soften. Spread sushi rice over the seaweed, leaving a 1 in (2.5 cm) border on the 2 long sides. Place thin strips of blanched vegetables or marinated fish lengthways in the center of the rice. Re-wet the exposed seaweed, and carefully roll length-ways, using the plastic wrap to help you. Chill until firm, then cut into 1 in (2.5 cm) slices and remove the plastic wrap. Serve with soy sauce and dabs of wasabi paste and ginger. One roll makes 8 pieces.

Meringue Yule Log

YULE WAS THE ANCIENT PAGAN FESTIVAL that celebrated the winter solstice. A feast prepared on the shortest day of the year preceded a period of celebrations, and the centerpiece of the festivities was a huge log for the fire called the yule log. Modern cooks have made the log deliciously edible. Traditionally, it is a chocolate roulade covered and filled with a thick chocolate frosting. This scrumptious alternative is a frozen coffee and chocolate mousse cake covered with warm coffee meringue. The hot, toasted exterior and the frozen interior are a wonderful contrast. To get the timing right on this recipe, make the mousse cake first. While it is in the freezer, make the meringue mushrooms (they need to be baked for 2 hours). Prepare the meringue for the log when you are ready to put the dessert in the oven. (This yule log should be eaten as soon as the meringue is golden.)

Woodland Setting
A woodland setting is the most natural decoration for a yule log. The dessert nestles in silvery lichen strewn with a few berries, dried leaves, pine cones, and mushrooms made from meringue. To make life easier, you can make the mousse cake and mushrooms up to two weeks in advance.

Autumn leaf

Pine cone

INGREDIENTS

Mousse Cake:

6 tbs (85 g) butter
⅓ cup (75 g) superfine sugar
3 large eggs
¾ cup (85 g) cocoa powder
¾ cup (175 ml) espresso coffee
½ cup (55 g) ground almonds
2 large egg whites

Meringue:

4 large egg whites
2 tsp instant coffee powder
¼ tsp cream of tartar
1½ cups (170 g) confectioners'
  sugar
2 oz (60 g) chocolate, melted

METHOD

Make the mousse cake: in a large bowl, beat the butter and sugar until creamy. Beat in the 3 whole eggs. In a small bowl, blend the cocoa powder and espresso coffee. Stir into the egg mixture with the ground almonds. Beat the 2 egg whites until stiff peaks form. Gently fold them into the egg mixture. Line a 9 x 5 in (23 x 13 cm) baking pan with buttered waxed paper and pour in the mix. Bake at 350° F (175° C) for 30 minutes.

When the mousse cake has cooled, turn it onto a board and peel off the paper. Trim 1 in (2.5 cm) off one long side and freeze.

Make the meringue mushrooms. Beat one of the egg whites, ½ tsp of the instant coffee powder, and a pinch of the cream of tartar until soft peaks form. Sift in ⅓ cup (40 g) of the confectioners' sugar, and beat until stiff peaks form. Transfer the meringue to a pastry bag with a ½ in (1.3 cm) nozzle. Pipe circles for the caps and lines for the stalks onto a baking sheet covered with waxed paper. Bake at 200° F

(95° C) for 2 hours. When cool, stick the stalks to the caps with melted chocolate.

Prepare the meringue for the yule log, using the rest of the egg whites, instant coffee powder, cream of tartar, and confectioners' sugar, following the instructions given above.

To assemble, place the frozen mousse cake on a baking sheet and cover with the meringue. With a small knife, swirl it to make a barklike texture and sculpt some broken branch ends. Bake at 425° F (220° C) for 8 minutes. Decorate and serve immediately.

• Meringue mushroom

• Silver lichen

• Mountain ash berry

FRUIT SAVARIN

IF YOU ARE SEARCHING for an absolutely spectacular dessert, here it is. This delectable ring of leavened cake is drenched in rum syrup and overflowing with luscious sticky, poached, and preserved fruit. Fresh fruit plus sprigs of sugared mint leaves and flowers add a final decorative flourish. The savarin looks so amazing that it seems a pity to make the first cut and dismantle it. However, once that first step is over, it should be easy to persuade guests to try a piece! This dessert has so many different flavors and textures to be shared and enjoyed: pears, figs, apricots, cherries, oranges, nuts, and profiteroles. Add them to the most moist cake imaginable and you can be sure that Fruit Savarin will become a Christmas regular.

FRUIT SAVARIN
Cake:
2 packages (30 g) active dry yeast
4 tbs sugar
1¼ cups (295 ml) lukewarm milk
4 cups (455 g) all-purpose flour
1 tsp salt
6 large eggs, at room temperature
1 stick (170 g) melted butter
Syrup:
2½ cups (590 ml) water
2 cups (455 g) superfine sugar
1 cup (235 ml) rum or kirsch
Decorations:
Wine-poached Pears (RIGHT)
Fresh fruit
Crystallized fruit (SEE
*   PAGES 38–39)*
Sugared flowers and mint leaves (SEE PAGES 82–83)
Caramel profiteroles and nuts (SEE PAGE 89)

Combine the yeast, sugar, and milk. Sift in the flour and salt, then beat in the eggs. Place in an oiled bowl, cover, and let rise in a warm place for 1 hour, until doubled in size. Punch down and mix in the melted butter. Stir vigorously for 7 minutes, until smooth and elastic. Butter and flour a 12 in (30 cm) savarin or ring mold. Pour in the batter. Cover and let rise in a warm place for 45 minutes. Bake at 375° F (190° C) for 35 minutes. Cover loosely with foil if it starts to brown too much.

Meanwhile, make the syrup. Vigorously boil the water and sugar for 20 minutes, until syrupy. After 5 minutes, add the rum or kirsch.

Remove the savarin from the oven and, after a few minutes, shake to loosen in its mold. Prick with a skewer, then pour half of the hot syrup over. When cold, turn onto an 18 in (46 cm) plate, fill with fruit, and decorate. Serve the remaining syrup separately. Serves 16.

Wine-poached Pear

Fresh fig

Crystallized pear half

Caramel nut

Fresh clementine •

• Caramel
profiterole

WINE-POACHED PEARS
1 bottle Beaujolais
2 cups (455 g) sugar
6 whole cloves
10 medium, firm pears
3 drops red food coloring
3 tbs blackberry brandy or
créme de cassis

Bring the wine, sugar, and
cloves to boil in a large
saucepan, then reduce to
a simmer. Peel the pears
(leaving the stems on), and
immediately place them in
the syrup. Simmer for about
15–20 minutes, until the
pears are translucent and
just tender. When cool,
add the food coloring and
alcohol. Leave overnight.
Remove the pears, and boil
the syrup to reduce by a
third. Spoon the syrup
over the pears to glaze.

• Crystallized
orange slice

• Crystallized
cherry

Crystallized •
apricot

Sugared primrose •

• Sugared
mint leaf

𝓕RUITY FEAST
A sumptuous rum-soaked
savarin heaped with
decorative fruit makes a
breathtaking dessert for
Christmas day dinner.
Guests can help themselves
to their favorite fruit.

TEMPLATES

ENLARGE THESE TEMPLATES to the size you require on a photocopier.
Use the enlarged image to give you an outline.

CHRISTMAS CHAINS

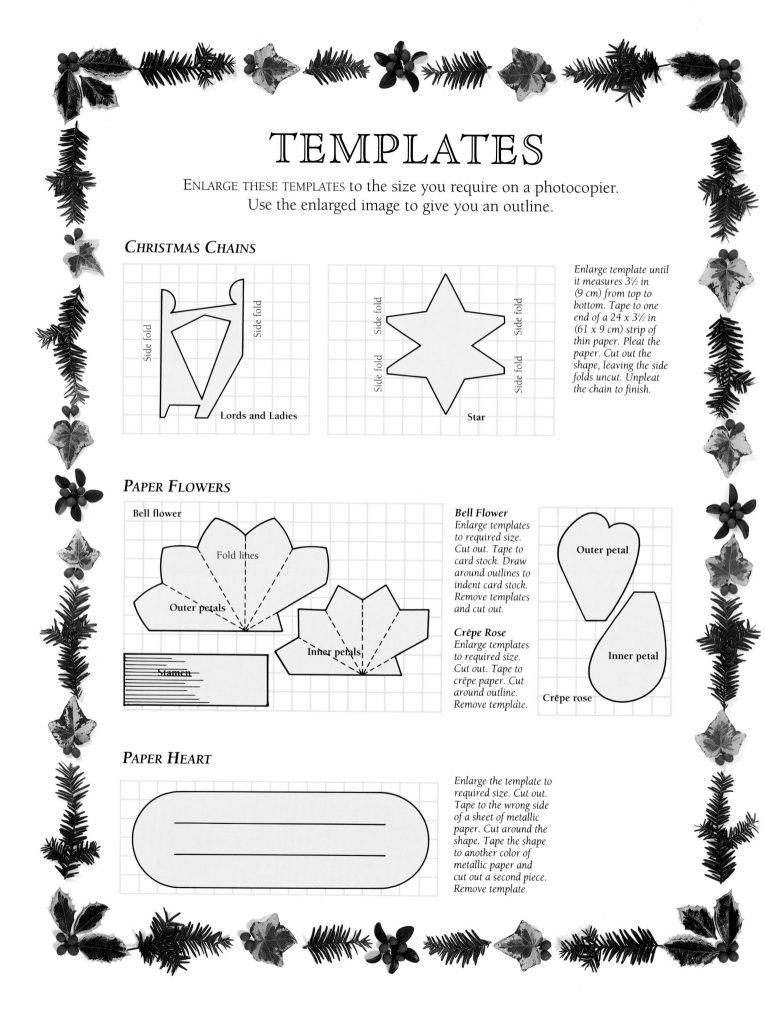

Side fold

Side fold

Lords and Ladies

Side fold

Side fold

Side fold

Side fold

Star

Enlarge template until it measures 3½ in (9 cm) from top to bottom. Tape to one end of a 24 x 3½ in (61 x 9 cm) strip of thin paper. Pleat the paper. Cut out the shape, leaving the side folds uncut. Unpleat the chain to finish.

PAPER FLOWERS

Bell flower

Fold lines

Outer petals

Inner petals

Stamen

Bell Flower
Enlarge templates to required size. Cut out. Tape to card stock. Draw around outlines to indent card stock. Remove templates and cut out.

Crêpe Rose
Enlarge templates to required size. Cut out. Tape to crêpe paper. Cut around outline. Remove template.

Outer petal

Inner petal

Crêpe rose

PAPER HEART

Enlarge the template to required size. Cut out. Tape to the wrong side of a sheet of metallic paper. Cut around the shape. Tape the shape to another color of metallic paper and cut out a second piece. Remove template.

GIFT BOXES

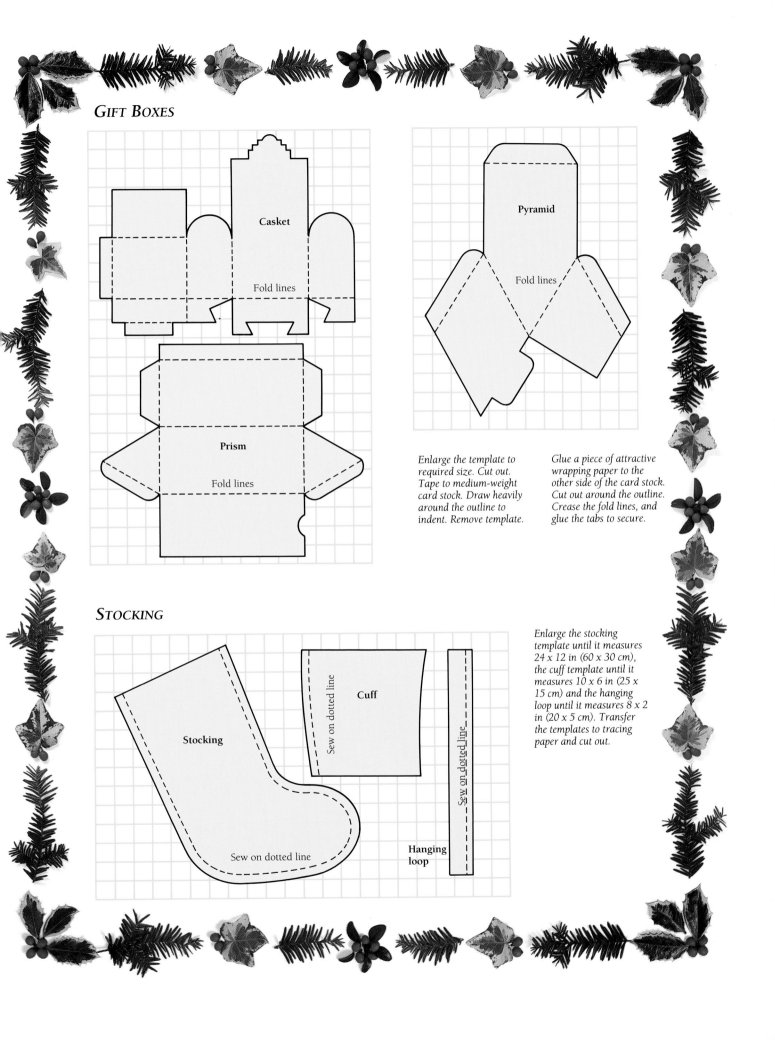

Casket

Fold lines

Prism

Fold lines

Pyramid

Fold lines

Enlarge the template to required size. Cut out. Tape to medium-weight card stock. Draw heavily around the outline to indent. Remove template.

Glue a piece of attractive wrapping paper to the other side of the card stock. Cut out around the outline. Crease the fold lines, and glue the tabs to secure.

STOCKING

Stocking

Sew on dotted line

Cuff

Sew on dotted line

Hanging loop

Sew on dotted line

Enlarge the stocking template until it measures 24 x 12 in (60 x 30 cm), the cuff template until it measures 10 x 6 in (25 x 15 cm) and the hanging loop until it measures 8 x 2 in (20 x 5 cm). Transfer the templates to tracing paper and cut out.

INDEX

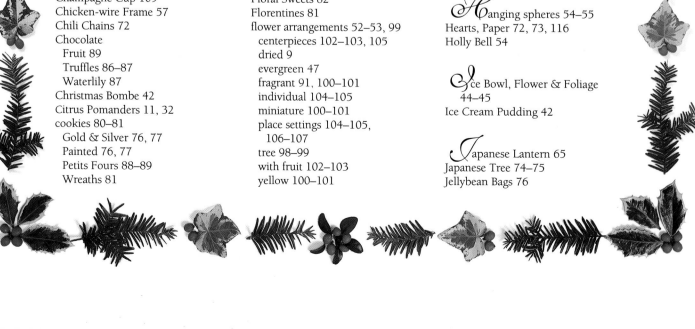

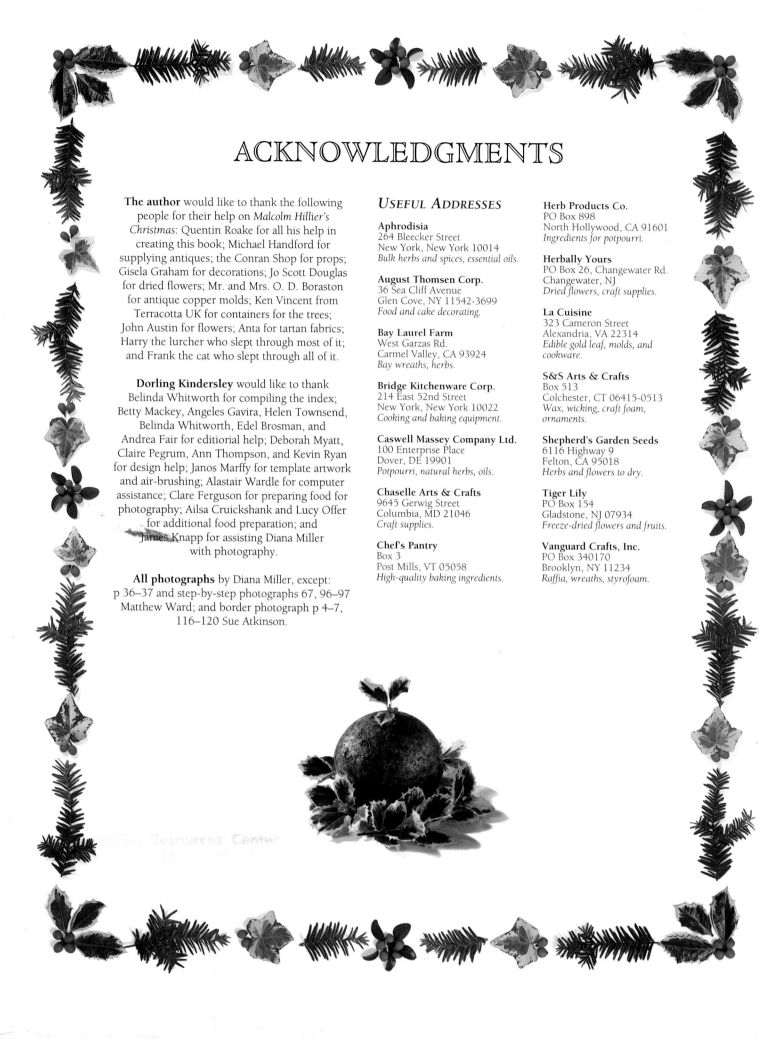

ACKNOWLEDGMENTS

The author would like to thank the following people for their help on *Malcolm Hillier's Christmas*: Quentin Roake for all his help in creating this book; Michael Handford for supplying antiques; the Conran Shop for props; Gisela Graham for decorations; Jo Scott Douglas for dried flowers; Mr. and Mrs. O. D. Boraston for antique copper molds; Ken Vincent from Terracotta UK for containers for the trees; John Austin for flowers; Anta for tartan fabrics; Harry the lurcher who slept through most of it; and Frank the cat who slept through all of it.

Dorling Kindersley would like to thank Belinda Whitworth for compiling the index; Betty Mackey, Angeles Gavira, Helen Townsend, Belinda Whitworth, Edel Brosman, and Andrea Fair for editiorial help; Deborah Myatt, Claire Pegrum, Ann Thompson, and Kevin Ryan for design help; Janos Marffy for template artwork and air-brushing; Alastair Wardle for computer assistance; Clare Ferguson for preparing food for photography; Ailsa Cruickshank and Lucy Offer for additional food preparation; and James Knapp for assisting Diana Miller with photography.

All photographs by Diana Miller, except: p 36–37 and step-by-step photographs 67, 96–97 Matthew Ward; and border photograph p 4–7, 116–120 Sue Atkinson.

USEFUL ADDRESSES

Aphrodisia
264 Bleecker Street
New York, New York 10014
Bulk herbs and spices, essential oils.

August Thomsen Corp.
36 Sea Cliff Avenue
Glen Cove, NY 11542-3699
Food and cake decorating.

Bay Laurel Farm
West Garzas Rd.
Carmel Valley, CA 93924
Bay wreaths, herbs.

Bridge Kitchenware Corp.
214 East 52nd Street
New York, New York 10022
Cooking and baking equipment.

Caswell Massey Company Ltd.
100 Enterprise Place
Dover, DE 19901
Potpourri, natural herbs, oils.

Chaselle Arts & Crafts
9645 Gerwig Street
Columbia, MD 21046
Craft supplies.

Chef's Pantry
Box 3
Post Mills, VT 05058
High-quality baking ingredients.

Herb Products Co.
PO Box 898
North Hollywood, CA 91601
Ingredients for potpourri.

Herbally Yours
PO Box 26, Changewater Rd.
Changewater, NJ
Dried flowers, craft supplies.

La Cuisine
323 Cameron Street
Alexandria, VA 22314
Edible gold leaf, molds, and cookware.

S&S Arts & Crafts
Box 513
Colchester, CT 06415-0513
Wax, wicking, craft foam, ornaments.

Shepherd's Garden Seeds
6116 Highway 9
Felton, CA 95018
Herbs and flowers to dry.

Tiger Lily
PO Box 154
Gladstone, NJ 07934
Freeze-dried flowers and fruits.

Vanguard Crafts, Inc.
PO Box 340170
Brooklyn, NY 11234
Raffia, wreaths, styrofoam.